# THE MODERN MOM'S
## Guide to Dads

# THE MODERN MOM'S
# Guide to
# Dads

## Ten Secrets Your Husband Won't Tell You

## Hogan Hilling, founder, Proud Dads Inc., and Jesse Jayne Rutherford

CUMBERLAND HOUSE
NASHVILLE, TENNESSEE

THE MODERN MOM'S GUIDE TO DADS
PUBLISHED BY CUMBERLAND HOUSE PUBLISHING
431 Harding Industrial Drive
Nashville, Tennessee 37211

Cover design: James Duncan Creative
Book design: Mary Sanford

**Library of Congress Cataloging-in-Publication Data**
Hilling, Hogan.
  The Modern mom's guide to dads : ten secrets your husband won't tell you / Hogan Hilling and Jesse Jayne Rutherford.
      p. cm.
  ISBN-13: 978-1-58182-606-7 (pbk. : alk. paper)
  ISBN-10: 1-58182-606-0 (pbk. : alk. paper)
  1. Fathers—Psychology. 2. Husbands—Psychology. 3. Mothers—Psychology. 4. Wives—Psychology. 5. Parenting. I. Rutherford, Jesse Jayne, 1977– II. Title.

HQ756.H558 2007
155.6'462—dc22

                                                    2007033931

Printed in Canada
1 2 3 4 5 6 7—13 12 11 10 09 08 07

# Contents

# Introduction

Have you ever scratched your head about your husband's parenting style? Have you and your husband ever fought over the differences in your parenting philosophies, or about how involved he should be as a dad? Have you ever wished you and your husband could parent as a team instead of as rivals?

If so, I've written this book for you. For the last sixteen years, I've been a stay-at-home dad; my wife, Tina, is a speech-language pathologist and I'm a full-time homemaker and dad to our three sons, Grant, Wesley, and Matt, who are now in their teens. Thanks to this role reversal, I experienced the difficulties of caring for kids and developed a new appreciation for parenting—both from moms' and dads' perspectives. My wife also experienced the challenges of this role reversal, and I'm forever grateful to her for her courage and flexibility.

In 1992, I was invited to give some workshops on fathering to local hospitals to share this perspective, and I later founded Proud Dads, Inc. as a formalization of these workshops. The purpose of my workshops has been to meet with new and expectant dads and provide a forum to discuss parenting in a place men could feel comfortable. Attendance was small at first, but the groups grew steadily over the years, confirming my belief that men could become more active parents and feel more entitled to discuss their true feelings about fatherhood.

Not long after I started Proud Dads, Inc., I got a surprise: I began to receive requests from moms to give workshops on fatherhood! Groups of moms invited me to come speak to them about what I learned from dads in my work. Soon, I found myself giving workshops to large groups of women like you who wanted to know more about what their husbands thought about being dads. They asked me questions like "Why doesn't my husband spend more time with the kids?" "Why am I stuck doing all of the housework?" and "How can I get my husband more involved with our family and household?" Meanwhile, in their own workshops, men were sharing the secret hopes, fears, frustrations, and desires that I describe in this book, and why they felt uncomfortable communicating them to their wives. After awhile, I felt like I was playing a game of Telephone between groups of moms and dads who couldn't communicate, or who had given up on it.

As of today, I've given more than two thousand workshops at hospitals, corporations, and conferences across the country, and it's been fascinating to hear both sides of the story. When the moms in my workshops began urging me to write a book about this experience, I realized it was a solution to this communication gap. I decided to write a book that answered moms' questions by telling them what dads have been confiding to me for over fifteen years.

This guide explains modern dads' behavior and how you can get your husband involved in the household without manipulating or nagging him so that you can parent as a team so that your marriage and your kids benefit. In every chapter, you'll find stories from my life and from other dads' lives that shed light on each secret dads keep from their wives, quotes from real dads about their feelings, helpful tips, and a section called "And a Mom Wants You to Know," written by my co-author and your contemporary mom, Jesse Jayne Rutherford. This book reveals ten secrets your husband won't tell you—but I will—in ten easy-to-read chapters that clarify your husband's behavior while respecting his feelings and the difficulties he faces. I call it a "Parenting Relationship" book, and I think you'll find it funny, heartwarming, and essential to you and your husband's success at raising kids together!

Best wishes,
Hogan Hilling

# OUR MARRIAGE COMES FIRST

I once knew a guy named Evan whose marriage had started to fall apart: after the baby came along, he and his wife lost touch, stopped communicating, and didn't make time to nurture their marriage. They put the baby first in every aspect of their lives. Evan came home from work as a real estate agent each night, exhausted, to a wife and baby who were equally exhausted. After a half-hour of griping at each other and frustration over holding a baby who cried whenever she was out of her mother's arms, Evan and his wife would retreat to different rooms and different activities.

As you can imagine, things started going downhill. Each night, Evan dreaded coming home, his wife dreaded seeing him, and his daughter squalled whenever he picked her up. Not long after the baby turned one, Evan didn't come home after work. Instead, he hired a prostitute downtown, then drove to a nearby hotel. And then . . . he started talking.

Evan later told me that while the prostitute sat on the bed, looking befuddled but understanding, he began venting about all of the stress, worries, and day-to-day annoyances he'd been experiencing at work and as a new dad over the past year, which he hadn't been able to share with his wife because they fought whenever they talked. Fully dressed in his slacks, shirt, and tie, Evan paced the room, running his hands through his hair. "The housing market is going down," he confided. "I keep trying to get better listings, but it's hard in a good market, and now what am I going to do? I can work harder to try and get ahead, but the market's against me." The prostitute listened and nodded.

After a couple of hours of talking, Evan realized he wasn't even interested in having sex with her, so he paid the prostitute and went home. He felt guilty for having hired a prostitute, but he was surprised at himself for not having had sex with her! He realized that while he wanted more sex in his life, he obviously had a greater need for intimacy in general, for emotional release, and for a chance to speak openly, none of which he had had at home since his daughter was born. He also needed to talk about his work worries.

Unfortunately, I've met other men who actually *have* cheated on their wives, with prostitutes, coworkers, or women they meet at bars. Infidelity, at least in the men I've worked with, usually happens when a man isn't getting something at home, and I don't mean just sex, as you can see from Evan's story, although that's part of it. I'm talking about *connectedness*. I'm talking about men's security in their role as husbands. I'm talking about the underlying vision men have of what make the foundation for a strong family: a strong marriage. And that's the first secret dads have shared with me over the years:

### Dads Feel That the Husband-Wife Relationship Has to Come Before the Parent-Child Relationship

Let me clarify that I'm not talking about physical safety: if the house is on fire, today's dads are still going to get the kids out first. Nor do a dad's needs come before a kid's needs: if Dad and Junior are both sleepy on the drive home, it's Junior who gets to conk out in his car seat.

What I'm talking about is the glue that holds a family together. We dads—and many moms, too—feel that having a strong marriage will prevent parents from getting divorced and will yield a happier home life for all involved. In addition, our kids will learn more about building relationships from how they see us treat and relate to our wives, which is another reason why it's so important for us to nurture our relationship with each other, even if it means changing some of our habits. As the kids become adults, it will matter less what they've absorbed from other people, what they see and witness mom and dad doing is what will determine their future behavior.

Please note that I'm not advocating that you stay in a bad marriage—I'm advocating that couples reinforce and nurture good marriages so that they don't become bad ones. How do we do this? The dads I've worked with over the years have given many suggestions that boil down to one simple rule:

### Make Time for Us as a Couple

Dads feel that they need more time with Mom, away from the kids. When I relay this message to the moms in some of my workgroups, some of them respond, "Are you crazy? I'm already being pulled in ten different directions! Can't my husband understand that I don't have time to pamper him, and even if I did, I might want to spend that time sleeping instead?"

I answer, "Yes, dads know that. They know you are wiped out, stressed, overworked, and feeling guilty." And then I explain to them what I'll tell you in Chapters 6, 7, and 8: dads are going to pick up the slack for you so that you can sleep, have some time alone, and still have time left over for your marriage!

For now, though, let's go back to square one: the foundation of your family. Do you remember how you used to be boyfriend and girlfriend? Free of responsibilities? How you used to go to the movies at the drop of a hat? Take a moment to remember what it was that brought you together in the first place. What was it about your husband that made you fall in love with him and want to marry him? What was it about you that he found attractive? Don't lose sight of these qualities or your love for each other. In my case, I married Tina because I thought she could make me a better person— it wasn't a purely physical attraction, and I'll bet most marriages aren't.

At some point, you were in love enough to make a commitment to each other. But the dynamic of the relationship probably changed when you made the transition from dating to marriage. That's when you started having to call or leave a note if you thought you'd be home late. But now, you're either a mom or a mom-to-be, and the dynamic is changing again. After the birth, you'll be bringing home more than a baby: you'll be bringing home a third person, a person with his or her own personality, likes, dislikes, opinions, and needs. As you know already from your marriage, loving someone takes hard work. Now you have another person to love! It's wonderful, and it's also harder for dads and moms.

One dad told me, "I'm struggling to keep an intimate relationship with my wife as it is. Now I'll have to start a new one with another human being. Juggling both scares me. I'm a bit unsure about my ability to handle two very personal relationships at one time."

As a father of three, I can tell you that this shift in family dynamics will happen again with each new baby that comes, but the love you and your husband have for each other should remain and even grow. You have to spend time alone together and paying attention to each other's needs in order for this to happen.

Dads feel it's very important to stay close to their wives. Here's what they have told me:

*I married my wife, not my kids. I love to spend time with my kids, but I also love to spend time alone with my wife.*

*It seems as though my wife is much more sensitive to her girlfriends' needs and feelings than she is to mine. She doesn't talk to me with the same level of compassion that she does to her girlfriends.*

*My wife spends more time trying to impress her boss, friends, and neighbors than she does me. When we go to a party, she'll spend hours putting on makeup and getting dressed. But when it comes time—which is rare—to have a romantic interlude with me in bed, there is no time or energy for it.*

*Our dog gets more attention than I do. My wife spends more time nurturing, petting, and cuddling the dog than she does me.*

*I don't think my wife knows or understands how rejected I feel when she says she doesn't want to have sex with me.*

*I need that physical contact with my wife. Not just the sexual intercourse, but the touching of skin to skin.*

These dads are saying that intimacy in their marriage is important to them. Okay, so is the sex. Men love sex, no two ways about it. For many of us, sex is intimacy and having sex with our wives is an important part of our lives that we don't want to lose, but that doesn't mean our wives should go through the motions just to please us. Despite loving sex, some men feel that having a strong libido is a burden, and talking about it with your husband can help you figure out how to find a happy medium. Don't be surprised if he has a hard time expressing his true emotions without using words women find offensive, and try to listen nonjudgmentally. If he feels you are disgusted or are going through the motions just to please him, it may put a damper on his ability to express himself and feel comfortable during sex.

There are, of course, some men whose sex drive goes down the tubes during and after pregnancy, and it's worth discussing here and with your husband. Dads have told me:

*Now, it's like I'm having sex with my child's mother and*

*not my wife. It just feels different. And it took me a while to get over it.*

*After watching my wife deliver our baby, I lost interest in having sex with her for a while. It had nothing to do with not loving my wife. But each time I thought about having sex, the first thing that popped into my mind was seeing our baby come out of her vagina. Putting my penis in the same place didn't seem all that appealing to me. It took several weeks to get over it.*

Notice, though, that these dads told me that they got over this lack of sex drive and never stopped loving their wives. If you think your husband has lost some interest in sex, ask him what's on his mind. He may have further fears about the safety of having sex during and after pregnancy that you can help him understand. It's a common misconception that sex during pregnancy will hurt the baby, so if you think your husband has fears about hurting you or the baby by having sex during pregnancy, get him in touch with some credible sources on the issue, like a pregnancy book or your doctor. Most men will quickly regain their sex drive, though, or else there would be few families with more than one child!

So even though sex is at the heart of romance for most men, it's not the be-all, end-all of their marriage. Ultimately, most dads love the mothers of their children. They feel it is imperative that they not neglect their marriage, so much so that they're willing to make time for you so that the two of you can spend more time together. (Where can you find this extra time? Read chapters 6, 7, and 8!)

## AND A MOM WANTS YOU TO KNOW

# More About Sex

What I hear Hogan and some of the other dads saying is that they want to have sex with their wives. I think it's crucial to understand how important sex is to our husbands. Does that mean we should feel obligated to have sex when we don't want to? No. Does that mean we should feel guilty for not wanting to? No. I think it is, however, important to have a frank discussion with your husband about sex and how the two of you feel about it. Be clear about what you want and don't want, your fears of getting pregnant if you don't want to have another baby, and how much time and energy you have for sex. Don't feel guilty about voicing your feelings. Then listen to his suggestions about how to combat some of these fears and solve some of the problems.

It is *very* important that you be honest about your feelings! Here's why. Let's say you don't want to have sex because it just doesn't sound appealing to you, but you tell your husband that you don't want to have sex because you don't have time for it. He would probably say, "Okay, I'll get the kids ready for bed at night so you can have some extra time. Problem solved!" Of course, if sex sounded unappealing to you, the problem would *not* be solved, and you'd have to find another excuse. He'd solve that problem, too, and after a while one of you would become frustrated and angry. So if sex is unappealing to you, say so. If your husband has a greater sex drive than you do, bring both of your needs out into the open and discuss them so that everyone's needs are addressed and you each know what to expect from the other.

## Respect a Boundary Between our Marriage and Other People

Dads feel that it's important that parents share authority and present a united front to the kids. In addition, it is important to maintain a boundary between their marriage and other people—even your own parents. Many dads feel it's important to maintain this boundary from the very beginning of your baby's life, starting with the delivery:

*My wife wanted her mom in the delivery room. Not me. I didn't even want my mother in there. I wanted this to be our moment, and I didn't want to share it with any of our relatives or friends. Her mom had already had this experience three times.*

*My wife wanted her mom to stay in our house for two weeks after the birth. I told her that I would rather have time alone with her and the baby. She got upset and accused me of being insensitive and not liking her mom. She made me feel like I was being selfish.*

*My wife and I came to a compromise. We made a list of rules and guidelines regarding help and visitors. We agreed to have her mom help out and visit us. However, we put her up in a hotel instead of having her stay with us. This way, we had control of when she could come over.*

*I have a great mother-in-law. I know her help will come in handy and that she'll have a calming effect on my wife. But I want to be the one that helps. Plus, I go back to work in three weeks and I want to make the best use of this time with my new family. And my wife needs to understand that this is our family and not her mother's family.*

Help is great, but it shouldn't interfere with your family bonding, and it should be just that: help. Your family should largely be able to function on its own if both you and your husband are present.

When our first child was born, I did something I'll always regret: I didn't follow my instincts about maintaining a boundary between our new family and the outside world. I felt that it was important for Tina, Grant, and me to spend time alone bonding, but I was overwhelmed by the number of phone calls and visits we had during the first six weeks of Grant's life. It was nice to have people come over to help, but it was also annoying to have the phone waking us up at three in the afternoon when we were all sleep-deprived and hadn't spoken to each other in more than a Cro-Magnon grunt in days.

After Grant was born, it seemed like Tina spent more time at her mom's house than she did at our house. There were several days when Grant was only a few weeks old that Tina went to her mom's place without me and stayed there all day. I understood her good intentions in doing so— respect and love for her mom, a need for comfort and advice on how to *be* a mom—but I felt excluded, abandoned, and useless. How could I bond with our baby and learn to take care of him if I couldn't see him? It was as if her relationship with her mom was more important than our marriage and our family time. Because of these days when I was left out, and because of the rush of guests when baby Grant was at home, there was little opportunity for Tina and me to learn how to work together as a parenting *team*.

I've spent the subsequent years telling expecting parents to take six weeks for bonding at the beginning of the baby's life. Urge your husband to take as much time off as possible during the first six weeks, and to use his vacation time if any is available. Let him take on the role of protector and nurturer during this time. His involvement will allow him to bond with the baby, help with childcare, and understand the difficulties of childcare so he can empathize later, especially if he is going back to work and you'll be doing the bulk of household work and childcare.

When the baby comes, turn off the ringer on the phone, and record a message on your voicemail with the pertinent info: "Hi, thanks for calling the Johnson Family! Brianna Rae Johnson was born on October 3 and she is healthy and happy. She weighed 8 pounds, 1 ounce, and is 19 inches long. Her parents are doing fine. If you would like to leave a message, please do so after the beep, and we'll return your call when we are back in the swing of things. Thanks!" That's what most people want to know, anyway.

If you include your husband in the first six weeks of the baby's life, he will understand how difficult it is to be a stay-at-home parent. He'll bond with the baby so that they have a strong relationship, which is good for all of you. If your husband goes back to work and you stay home, he won't take for granted what you've done all day with the baby. He'll understand what you're going through.

Absent an abusive, miserable relationship, dads, like psychologists and other experts, widely agree that intact marriages are the best environments for raising healthy, happy kids. One dad used the Airplane Oxygen Mask Analogy to explain why he felt his marriage had to come before his relationship with his kids:

*On an airplane, the flight attendant shows you how to put on an oxygen mask in case of emergency. Then they tell you what to do if your kid is with you: first put your mask on, then put the kid's mask on. That's because you can only help your kid if you're alive! I think this applies to my marriage—first we build a strong foundation, and from there we raise our kids.*

I love my kids. I love my wife. In fact, I love her more than I did when we got married, and it's because we've nurtured our marriage. I want to spend time alone with her—whether it's sharing a pizza and a bottle of wine on the beach, renting a movie, or having sex—so that we can maintain our marriage and our family.

**Hogan's Slogan #109:**
**Love isn't solid—it's more like clay than a rock.**

There's a song about love being solid as a rock, but I don't think love is solid. I think marriage is more like clay than a rock. Both Mom and Dad have to be flexible. Many people go into relationships saying, "This is who I am. Take it or leave it." Tina and I have learned that there's always room for improvement.

## Dad's Play-by-Play: What to Know from Chapter 1

- The marriage has to be strong and healthy for your family to stay intact, so spend some of your free time (you'll have free time after Chapters 6, 7, and 8) alone with your husband.

- Have at least one date a month.

- Have a frank discussion with your husband about sex, and listen nonjudgmentally.

- Create a boundary between your marriage and other people.

- Urge your husband to take off as much time as possible during the baby's first six weeks of life—this will give him a chance to bond with the baby and to take part in the childcare and household duties.

- Leave a recorded message on your voicemail with pertinent information after a new baby arrives, and turn the telephone ringer off.

- Set rules and guidelines for visitation from relatives, friends, and neighbors, including whether people will stay at your home or a hotel, and how long they will stay.

# THE BIRTH AND PREGNANCY ARE A BIG DEAL FOR US, TOO—HERE'S WHY

**Note:** *Your kids may already be walking and talking. If that's the case, read this chapter for historical perspective on your husband's behavior.*

**D**o you wish your husband would share his feelings with you more? Join the crowd! This is one of the most common complaints women have about their husbands. They wonder, *Why do men clam up and isolate themselves from the pregnancy?* Well, it's mostly because of the pent-up feelings I'll discuss in this chapter.

Guys often feel they're simply not allowed to share these feelings because talking about feelings is either not "manly," or because they're not supposed to burden you while you're dealing with the pregnancy. You can help by gaining an understanding of the feelings discussed in this chapter and by encouraging his involvement and expression of feelings.

Here's the first one:

## We Feel Responsible

Oh, man. Pregnancy is all our fault. A loving husband often says to himself during pregnancy, "Jeez, here's my lovely wife, puking nonstop; she can't sleep at night, her back is killing her, her hair's falling out, and the only relief she'll get from this pregnancy is through an excruciating childbirth! What have I done to her?"

But it doesn't stop there. Seeing his wife needs extra help and that he's in a position to protect her, the expectant dad will often feel it's his obligation to make sure the pregnancy and birth go off without a hitch. *What if something bad happens to my wife during pregnancy?* he thinks. *What if I'm so nervous that I get in a wreck while driving my wife to the hospital while she's in labor? What if the baby comes so fast that I have to deliver it myself? What if my wife dies? What if the baby dies? Why, oh why didn't I become a doctor?*

Don't laugh. These fears run through every guy's head, I can tell you. In one of the Proud Dads workshops, there was a guy named Daniel who asked me what to do if he had to deliver the baby himself.

"Don't worry," I answered. "You'll have plenty of time to get to the hospital. Labor is a long process."

"That's right," a new dad chimed in, rocking his infant son. "My wife was in labor for thirty hours!"

"My brother's wife was in labor for sixteen hours," someone else said. "He said that was long enough!"

"But wait," Daniel said. "Let's just say that I have to do it! What should I do?"

"Call a neighbor," somebody advised.

"Call a doctor," someone else added.

"No, call an *ambulance*," said a third person, and we all laughed.

Everyone, that is, except Daniel. He stood up and threw open his hands. "But what if *I* have to deliver the baby? Let's just say we're stuck in rush-hour traffic on the way to the hospital! Let's just say her labor is really fast! Let's just say I have to deliver the baby myself! *What am I supposed to do?*"

We all got quiet and looked at Daniel. I realized that all of his fears about childbirth had narrowed down to this one "what if?" and that he had gotten really freaked out thinking about it. He wanted to know how to deliver a baby, and he wasn't going to feel better until he had some pointers, regardless of the fact that he'd probably never use them. Somebody finally told him that he could look it up in the back of several different pregnancy books, like *What to Expect When You're Expecting*. "Do you think my wife has that book?" he asked.

"Oh, yeah," I said. "You should really flip through it." (Notice I told him to flip through it, not read it. Asking a guy who is already stressed to read five-hundred-plus pages might be a little overwhelming. Just flag some key pages for him to get him comfortable with the subject.)

Truly, though, the source of Daniel's fear was not the possibility of delivering the baby, nor was it a lack of knowledge about pregnancy and childbirth. It was actually his sense of responsibility for his wife's and baby's safety during the most important and dangerous task he'd have during the pregnancy: driving her to the hospital.

Other dads have confessed their fears in an all-male forum. Here's what they have shared with me:

*My fear is about not knowing what to do. What do I do when our baby cries and my wife's not around?*

*I wouldn't say this to my wife because I don't want to undermine what she's going through with the pregnancy, but this is no piece of cake for me, either. I'm really stressed out and exhausted.*

*I'm afraid that I won't meet my wife's standards and expectations. And also that I will let our son down by not knowing what his needs are.*

*I'm afraid there will be something wrong with our baby.*

*This sounds dumb, but I'm overwhelmed by all of the medical terms I have to learn right now. It takes longer to absorb the information in the pregnancy books when I'm not familiar with the vocabulary.*

*I keep worrying that I'll miss the birth. That I'll be at work and my wife won't be able to reach me, and she'll have to go to the hospital without me.*

*I'm afraid to be alone with our baby.*

*I'm afraid something will go wrong and my wife or baby will die in childbirth.*

Personally, when Tina was pregnant the first time, I admit I was terrified. She'd ask me if I was excited, and I'd fake like I was. Like a lot of guys, I'd been taught not to show much emotion, and I wanted to remain levelheaded until I had all of the facts—in this case, until the baby was actually born. Yeah, I was a little excited, but I was scared, too, because I'd never had a father in my life and I didn't know what to do or who to turn to. (This was in 1987, and there were no resources around for dads.)

Truth be told, another part of me was indifferent to the

pregnancy, just as Tina suspected. I wanted a baby not so much because I wanted to be a father, but because Tina wanted to be a mother so badly. I wanted parenthood for her sake. Even though I was stressed because I wanted everything to be perfect for her, I was asking myself, *Do I really want to be a dad?* In my first book, I wrote how Tina glowed and smiled when she held Grant for the first time, but when I held him for the first time, my heart sank. You see, I was scared out of my mind. I had no idea how I was supposed to act, what I was supposed to be doing, or how to take on my role as a father.

Over time, I grew as a father and when our second and third sons were born, I realized why I'd had a lack of connection with Grant before he was born: I just didn't have the vested interest in him that Tina had had. I hadn't been preparing mentally like Tina had been doing. I was more prepared for the birth of our second son, Wesley, and felt more of a bond with him. After he was born and we found out that he had a genetic disorder called Angelman Syndrome, I developed a really strong bond with him because I knew I had to help him and because I was now in a childcare role all the time—taking care of him and Grant at once was just too much for Tina. Because Wesley spent most of his time at the hospital the first three years of his life, one of us was always needed at the hospital while the other was at home caring for Grant. It was around this time that I began to realize the joys of parenting and I became the stay-at-home parent. We agreed that I would stay home for three years.

Let me tell you, on the first day that Tina went back to work and I found myself in the house with a three-year-old and an infant, I started counting off the days on the calendar until those three years were up! I may have witnessed the joys of parenting, but I didn't think I wanted to have them all the time; I wanted to do my time and get back out to the workforce, away from diapers, preschool, and spilled milk. Well, there was no use crying over it. I had to stick it out.

Soon, I changed my tune. I guess I had an epiphany.

I began to understand why moms choose to stay home with their kids. What an amazing experience! What precious moments I shared with my sons! I wouldn't trade my time with them for all the money in the world. These touching experiences were the subject of my first book. I finally had the connection with my kids that had been missing when Tina was pregnant with Grant.

The last step in this evolution took place when we started talking about a third child. Because Wesley's disability was pretty severe, we thought it would be healthy for Grant to have another sibling to form a relationship with. From the moment we found out Tina was pregnant for the third time, my whole attitude toward the baby was different because I knew that I'd be his primary caretaker from the moment he was born. I love all three of my sons equally, but my connection with Matt is strongest because I was more in tune with him from the moment he was conceived.

## We Are Afraid and Intimidated, But Can't Express It

I've found through my work that most dads experience the fear, worry, and indifference I felt during the first pregnancy.

It's a slam-dunk that your husband has fears of this type, too. Of course, so do you—you're probably also afraid of stepping into your new role as a mother and making sure your kids have what they need. It's a big job, no matter how much your finances, family, or friends can help with it.

But keep in mind that as a mom, you're allowed more of an outlet for your fears because your friends and family will not consider you "unwomanly" if you express those feelings. If a woman confided her fears to a female friend, the friend would probably put her arm around her, but guys don't console each other like that. What's more, you can counterbalance talking about your fears of motherhood by talking about the delights of motherhood with other women and with your husband. No one is going to call you a sissy or a wimp if you say, "Little Tyler fell asleep on my chest today! It was so sweet—he has the most perfect, tiny hands." Your husband may experience some of the same deep, tender feelings you do, but imagine him saying that to his buddies! He'd be laughed out of town, made to feel less of a man, or else completely ignored. For your husband, a best-case scenario would be for his friends to change the subject because they just don't want to go there. First there would be an uncomfortable silence, and then someone would say, "Uh, right . . . so, what did you think about that *Monday Night Football* game?"

There are hardly any books or classes for dads: across the country, the services for new and expectant moms far outnumber those for dads, which is why I've dedicated my work to helping fill this gap for dads. In the parenting section of any bookstore, you'll find the shelves stuffed with books geared toward moms, but hardly any for dads. A few years ago, I conducted a survey of 2,000 hospitals via e-mail to find out if they had programs for dads. Of those, 392 responded to the survey. Of those that responded to the survey, only 87 had any programs for fathers in place—less than one-fourth of all the hospitals that actually responded.

Over the years, I have called up hospitals across the country to see if we could start some programs for expectant dads. "No," I was told over and over again. "We have childbirth classes for both parents." (Incidentally, guys have told me that their favorite parts of the Lamaze classes and other childbirth programs are the bathroom breaks: the time when they can talk to other guys about what they're going through.) Some of the instructors I talked to liked the idea of having a class for dads; others, already overworked, resisted the idea of piling more tasks on their plate. I applaud those instructors who have gone the extra mile to secure classes like these for their organizations—it hasn't been easy for them.

Mostly, my efforts would play out like this conversation I had with an instructor:

"You see, I've been asked to provide some expectant father workshops in your area," I explained. "I think that the men *and* women feel it's really necessary."

The childbirth instructor laughed. "Guys don't want to take these classes," she scoffed. "They don't even ask questions in the childbirth classes we currently offer!"

"Probably because they're afraid of getting their egos bruised," I told her. "They feel embarrassed to ask basic questions and they don't want to hurt their wives' feelings if they admit they're afraid during the pregnancy. They even think that if they say something to upset their wives, and their wives start crying, it will affect the baby!"

"Hmm," she said. "That never crossed my mind."

I went on. "Guys do not want to share their feelings in a room full of pregnant women they don't even know. That would be like asking a woman to share her diary with a group of men she doesn't know. In the childbirth classes, the dads are usually just helpers and the content is focused on the physical mechanics of birth. Guys don't need help with that part. What they need is to talk about specific father-related issues that moms and childbirth instructors, who are usually women, haven't been through. What makes the class dynamic even more uncomfortable for men is that they aren't addressed as dads, they're addressed as *coaches*!"

"That's so no one gets their feelings hurt if the dad's not in the picture," the instructor told me.

"That's very sensitive to any moms who might be going through a breakup with their husbands or boyfriends," I replied. "But I'd bet that 95 percent of the 'coaches' in your classes really are the fathers of those babies, so you're alienating a larger part of your patients by leaving out the people who really are the dads. They need to be acknowledged for their commitment as husbands and for their future role as dads. How else are they going to feel like it's okay to ask questions and be a part of what's going on?"

"Look, Hogan," she said with a tired sigh. "I see your point, but unfortunately I'm not in the position to make any decisions. I can bring this up with my administration, but I have a feeling they're going to say no."

"Why?" I asked.

"We just don't have the budget for something like this," she answered.

I pointed out that hospitals across the country have money for childbirth classes for mothers, siblings, and even grandparents, but not for fathers. Didn't the hospital feel that fathers played a more vital role in the well-being of their families than siblings and grandparents?

"I went to a meeting with some colleagues in other states who actually have secured funds for fathering classes," the instructor told me. "But you know what? The classes folded!"

"How come?" I asked.

"They only had an average of five or six guys attending. Classes like these need more attendees to come out in the black financially."

I've done workshops for as few dads as one at a time! My philosophy is, if I help just one person, I've made progress. While a small class size wouldn't deter me, I know that hospitals run differently, so I didn't tell the instructor what my approach would be. Instead, I asked, "How long were the classes running?"

"Oh, five or six months," she answered.

I wanted to throw up my hands. What did they expect? This kind of class needs to spread not only by marketing, but by word of mouth. A cultural shift doesn't happen overnight. I asked her to please try talking to the administration and to let me know what they said.

That particular administration said no, but many others have said yes. One factor in improving the situation has been *moms'* advocacy for these programs. When fifteen or twenty moms get together and request classes for dads, the hospitals usually listen. Don't underestimate your power in getting hospitals to have classes and getting husbands to attend them. I'll discuss this more in Chapter 10. As one guy said with an embarrassed chuckle:

*I came to this dads' class because my wife made me. I really didn't want to come, but after listening to other*

*dads, I don't feel alone. I'm glad I came today—I'll have
to thank my wife when I get home.*

Great progress is being made: though only about 23 percent of hospitals currently offer programs for fathers, that number was virtually nil around the time my own kids were born.

Whether or not there are classes available in your area, you can still aid in supporting your husband as he makes this transition.

While you're pregnant, your husband may feel more comfortable opening up to some other men who are already fathers, so you could help by suggesting he hook up with another expectant dad, or a dad with young kids. Your husband may have met a guy he could be friends with at your childbirth class, and they may have even exchanged phone numbers, but since they're guys, they've probably never called each other! You can help by exchanging numbers with other moms, then trying to hook your husbands up so they get a chance to hang out. Remind him that he needs time to talk to other dads. In a one-on-one situation, or with other men who are involved dads, he may be more comfortable talking, or at least listening to someone else talk. Or you could invite some other parents over for dinner and let the dads talk about their perspectives on childbirth. They might want to do this away from the women; let them go out on the patio together and talk quietly. The next time they hang out, they might wish to go someplace by themselves so that they can talk more freely, and that's okay—he might need to take this in baby steps. Don't push him farther than he wants to go.

If you want to get your husband to share his feelings with you as well as with other men, then you must share some parenting activities with him, starting right now. Otherwise, he'll probably take on a grin-and-bear-it, stiff-upper-lip attitude toward parenting for the rest of his life. He'll think, "I'm the protector. I'm the tough guy. I've got to stuff all of my own feelings for my family's sake." While that's a pretty brave and noble attitude, it might not be the best tactic for the long haul. Validating his feelings and encouraging his involvement by asking him to participate is a good start toward effective communication habits and strong team parenting. Here are some activities you can involve your husband in:

- Prenatal check-ups—he probably can't make all of them, but he should be there for some. Remind him that the doctor works for you and that he should talk to the doctor and ask as many questions as he wants. Make sure the doctor includes your husband in the conversation and answers his questions.
- Light exercise with you, like walking around the block together and talking about the baby.
- Pregnancy updates. You can point to a page in your pregnancy book and say, "See, here's where we are right now. Look! The baby is the size of your thumb!" That can help the pregnancy seem like more of a reality for him.
- The sonogram—it's so cool! Of all the check-ups you go to, don't let him miss this one!
- Birthing classes (remember that he's the *dad*, not the "coach").
- The baby shower registry and the baby shower (as you'll see in Chapter 6, he might be more willing to use baby care items if he's involved in picking them out).
- Assembly, preparation, and trial runs of new equipment

like car seats, strollers, cribs, swings, high chairs, bottle warmers, etc. Ask him to put a bottle together and practice warming it up now so it's less stressful later.

- The birth! This might include cutting the umbilical cord, which is a big deal for a lot of guys.
- The lactation consultation at the hospital. If he listens to what the consultant says, he'll be more encouraging later and probably less likely to offer ineffective suggestions.
- When he does open up to you about his feelings, give him your attention.

Keep in mind that allowing fathers into the delivery room is a fairly new practice. Your husband may feel intimidated by what has always been considered a woman's domain, and his father may not have been present for births. Letting your husband take a tour of the labor and delivery ward ahead of time can help him feel more comfortable with his role when it comes time for the birth. Otherwise, he may say things like this:

*I was intimidated by all the machines in the delivery room. I was clueless as to what to do or what was going on. I felt I had no control over the situation.*

*Initially, I didn't want to be in the delivery room. I had a hard time explaining to my wife how the idea of watching her in pain and the sight of blood didn't appeal to me.*

*What if something goes wrong in the delivery room? What if I get in the way of the doctor's efforts to take care of our baby?*

Most hospitals today welcome dads in the delivery room and even have guided tours set up once a week for expectant parents. In fact, many childbirth instructors have told me they welcome dads to visit on their own. Take advantage of this service! Your husband (and probably you, too) will gain confidence and know where to go and what to do when the big day comes. By gaining confidence and worrying less about what's going on, your husband will be in a better position to be emotionally present for the birth.

When the baby is born, don't underestimate the importance of cutting the umbilical cord if your husband tells you he wants to do it. Make sure one of you tells the doctor before, during, and after the birth that he really wants to do this, because doctors can forget. Here is what one father, Pablo, told me about his experience in the delivery room.

Pablo and his wife were very excited about their new baby, and he was looking forward to cutting the umbilical cord. Cutting the umbilical cord was an event that would symbolize, in his mind, the beginning of his relationship with his son. Of course he'd been involved during the pregnancy, but he didn't feel like he'd had the opportunity for bonding that his wife had experienced. So he and his wife told the doctor that Pablo wanted to cut the umbilical cord, and the doctor agreed.

Cut to the delivery room, no pun intended. Pablo's wife was in labor for eleven hours, and then the baby was finally born! As Pablo stood by, holding his wife's hand, the doctor delivered the baby and handed him to a nurse so the nurse could start the routine of washing and cleaning the baby. They moved quickly. The doctor reached for the scissors and picked up the umbilical cord in her other hand. *Wait!* Pablo thought. *I wanted to do that!* He watched the scissors open. *What should I do?* he wondered. *Once it's cut, it's over!*

"Stop!" he yelled. The doctor looked up. "I want to cut the umbilical cord!" he shouted, reaching his hand out for the scissors.

"Oh," the doctor said, "you're absolutely right. I'm so sorry, go ahead." She handed him the scissors and stepped aside. Feeling nervous, he took a deep breath and then did the honors.

Later, the doctor told him, "I'm so glad you spoke up and stopped me. I'm in the habit of cutting the cords myself, and I completely forgot."

As it turned out, there was a dads' workshop later that day in the same hospital where Pablo's baby was born, and he dropped in for ten minutes to tell the dads-to-be how excited he was, and also to recommend that they cut their babies' umbilical cords. "If I hadn't spoken up," he told us, "I would have always regretted it. I think it would have definitely made a difference in how I see myself starting out as a father, and my wife wouldn't have understood that. Bye!" he said, and dashed back to the labor and delivery ward.

For many guys, cutting the umbilical cord is a huge deal—it's like setting the baby free from mom's womb. It symbolizes, "You've gotten to know Mom pretty well these last few months, now it's time for me to start a relationship with you, too." Your husband may not have given the umbilical cord much consideration, or he may not feel strongly about cutting it. There are even some guys are so squeamish about birth that they'd probably pass out. But if your husband is even mildly interested in cutting the umbilical cord, tell your doctor that he wants to do it and be sure to speak up if this event is forgotten during the action. It will be the one part of the birth that will be all his, and doing it can improve how he sees himself as an involved dad.

---

## ♀AND A MOM WANTS YOU TO KNOW
### More About Assembly of Baby Gear

I think Hogan has a great point about letting your husband assemble and try out all of the new baby gear. For one thing, it's totally okay for even the most macho of manly men to roll up his sleeves, get out the Allen wrenches, and put a crib together. For another thing, there is no way you'll want to do those things yourself while you're seven months pregnant.

But more importantly, letting your husband put a swing together, set it up in the baby's room in a place of his choosing, and make sure it's got the right batteries is going to make him feel useful, involved, and . . . *dadly.* And he'll probably be more apt to use the swing when he's alone with the baby instead of calling you on your cell phone and saying, "He won't stop crying. What should I do?"

My husband felt great pride in teaching me how to use the bottle warmer. I had never used it because I breastfed whenever I was with my daughter, but I needed to learn how to use it so I could teach my mom, who was coming to babysit.

"I've got a whole system," my husband explained, showing me the area on the counter we'd reserved for bottles and the bottle warmer. "Add water to the warmer, but don't add as much as it calls for, or the warmer takes *forever.* You only need to leave the bottle in it for about a minute; that's plenty of time. Then just check it on your wrist like this." He demonstrated. When he was done, he put his hands on his hips and grinned.

I think that the opportunity to teach me a parenting skill made him feel like he was helpful instead of in the way. And it *was* helpful—I wouldn't have had any freedom or break from breastfeeding if he hadn't taken on some of the childcare.

## We Feel Helpless When We See You in Pain

When someone you love is hurting, how do you feel? Awful, right? I know that when Tina is sick or the boys have hurt themselves, I have this undercurrent of sadness and helplessness beneath whatever other feelings I have going on at the time. Whether it's a cold or a broken arm, I'm angry that I have to settle for the role of protector because I can't make the pain go away.

Now imagine that your husband had to go through labor. Imagine it was your husband who had to go through all the pain of childbirth or a Cesarean and breastfeeding to boot. Imagine that he was crying out your name in pain.

Now that you're done laughing, let's be serious. It's a scene that's been mimicked in countless campy movies, I know. But all jokes aside, how would you feel if the man you loved were in some kind of horrible pain and your role was to just, well, stand there?

For one thing, you'd be frustrated. For another thing, you'd be ten steps behind when it came to adjusting and getting things in perspective. Let me tell you what I mean.

Of these two situations, I think the frustration might be easier to understand: most guys are used to being the tough ones in the family, and they're demoted to hand-holding while their wives are screaming. Other than epidurals, there's not much to be done about that. Most guys who have seen their wives give birth will come back to class and say something like, "Man, I have so much more respect for my wife now that I've seen what she went through. She's so tough!" A statement like this is a sign that your husband is growing emotionally. It has the added benefit of making you more attractive to your husband when you probably feel, as some of the moms in my workshops have said, "like a cow." Call it marriage insurance.

Now I'll explain about your husband being a few steps behind you in terms of perspective. I am forever grateful to Tina for being patient with me when I said the wrong thing at the wrong time just after Grant, our oldest son, was born. I was clueless and overwhelmed. In less than a year, I had gotten married, picked up a mortgage, and had a kid.

After Tina struggled through labor and experienced the first poignant moments of breastfeeding, we stayed up through the night at the hospital. When it was time to finally take my wife and new baby home, I wandered, zombie-like, out to the parking lot and pulled the car up to the hospital entrance. A nurse had wheeled Tina and Grant out to the curb in a wheelchair, where all of them were waiting for me. The nurse checked to see that we had a car seat for Grant, and then I took Grant awkwardly and opened the passenger's side door so Tina could get in. She tried to get comfortable so she could put her seatbelt on, but she was in a lot of pain. I was left to put Grant into his car seat.

*Uhhh . . .* I thought.

I wasn't sure what to do. I looked over my shoulder at the nurse for help, but she stepped back, saying that she couldn't put Grant in his car seat for liability reasons. It suddenly hit me that a baby is a non-returnable item, and for the first time, I became fully aware that I was a dad. The engine idled, as did my brain, and Tina fidgeted in the front seat. Grant's head wobbled as I sat him back in his new car seat, and I stifled a "Whoops!" as I got his little foot tangled up in his blanket. Oh, right. I'd have to unwrap him from the blanket *first*, and *then* put him in his car seat. Okay. Jeez, what if I hurt him? I'd had no training in fatherhood—forget about expectant father classes, I hadn't even had a dad around during my childhood that I could talk to or learn from. What was I doing with a baby in my arms? It was all too much for me. I was sweating bullets and near tears. "This is really hard," I confessed to Tina. I didn't necessarily mean that putting Grant into his car seat was hard, although it was. What I meant was that I was grappling with the whole concept of fatherhood, right then and there.

She gingerly turned around and our eyes met between the seats. Both of her eyes were bloodshot and puffy from labor. Then she turned back around without saying a word.

I realized later that the circumstances weren't right for me to say what I did. Not that it wasn't true. Putting Grant in his car seat *was* really hard for me, and I was just expressing my emotions. But I had not thought to put my situation in perspective, and I see now that it was completely insensitive. To her everlasting credit, Tina didn't smack me upside the head. A few months later, she told me she'd known *exactly* what she wanted to say to me, but she'd resisted.

"Oh, really?" I said, with a touch of sarcasm in my voice. "I thought you said you want me to be honest with you and share my feelings."

"Yeah, but it wasn't the right time."

She was right, of course, but when Grant was an infant, we were too emotional and overwhelmed to see straight, let alone communicate well. Plus, we hadn't had much practice communicating. Nowadays, I try to realize when it's the right time to talk and when it's not, and Tina and I both try to listen to each other's feelings, give each other a hug, and not set about fixing the other person's problems or offering advice.

This anecdote is probably best kept a secret, but I'm dragging it out so that you can see that your husband feels pretty helpless about his role in the birth process, and it can leave him feeling frustrated or else leave him light-years behind you in terms of perspective. The best thing to do is to involve him as much as possible, give him a little time to catch up to you in terms of growth, and listen when he does venture to express himself. He's got a tough row to hoe, as you'll see in the next chapter. But one more thing about newborns:

## We Are Also Tired, Stressed, and Overwhelmed After the Birth

While men admit they can't hold a candle to the physical pain and exhaustion their wives undergo after childbirth, they may also be tired, stressed, and overwhelmed during the pregnancy and when the new baby arrives. While your needs and the baby's physical needs may be the most pressing, don't forget to ask your husband how he's doing once in awhile, or even prompt relatives and friends to ask how he's doing. Taking on a new role as a dad is even more stressful when the world doesn't acknowledge your part in the play. As a mom, you can also reply how both of you are doing when people ask how you're doing as a mom. The point is to acknowledge that your husband is a dad and has a place in the family.

Other fathers have told me of their frustration with the way parenting correspondence is addressed in the mail, and I sympathize with them. After each of our children were born, we would receive a slew of magazines and baby gear advertisements in the mail, all of it addressed to *Mrs. Hilling*. More often than not, I was the person at home, I was the one to check the mail, and I would open those magazines and think, "What am I, chopped liver?" I take issue with parenting magazines that only address moms—it makes dads feel like parenting is none of their business. So if you're subscribing to a parenting magazine, look for one that recognizes fathers as a part of their readership so that your husband feels like it's okay for him to pick up the magazine and flip through it. Also, you can include his name on the subscription so that he's reminded of his role in the family each month that the magazine arrives. As you'll see in the next chapter, guys can get so caught up in their other duties as fathers that these monthly reminders can be helpful.

Even though your husband might be ten steps behind you in terms of adjusting, he's still adjusting, and it's going to be hard. Also, keep in mind that about 10 percent of new dads experience postpartum depression, and depression can be debilitating. Many times, depression can result from changes in lifestyle and loss of an old identity, discomfort with a new one, and the big issue, finances, which we'll get to soon.

Forming a team parenting relationship starts now, so give him space and permission to gripe a little. If he says, "I'm really tired," don't snap back, "Well, how do you think

I feel?" He may not be *as* tired as you, but if you want to parent as a team, and if you want him to open up to you, you need to let him gripe sometimes. Try saying, "It sounds like you're pretty tired. Why don't you go take a nap?" He might do so, he might not, but the point is that you've noticed and acknowledged that he is tired. Instead of resting, he might decide to start working really hard. When faced with a challenging situation, dads usually make the right decision, but when they don't, they learn from their mistakes and grow.

If he says, "I wish I could get a break," let him get out of the house so he can clear his head, even if all he does is go to the drugstore. When he comes back, ask him if he feels better. Listen to what he says.

But the main reason that dads feel tired, stressed, and overwhelmed after the birth is not because they're physically tired, but because they're mentally exhausted. The mental exhaustion is due to a reason that they may never tell you, at least not in so many words. I'll give it my full attention in Chapter Three, but here it is:

He fears he will not be able to provide financially for his family.

**Hogan's Slogan #41: "Men are very afraid that they will not be able to provide for their families."**

*Tread lightly.* This is an extremely delicate subject for most guys and, in terms of how they see themselves as mature men, it's equivalent to how they feel about penis size while on the dating scene. Let's discuss the role of provider in more detail—read on.

## Dad's Play-by-Play: What to Know from Chapter 2

- Your husband feels responsible for the pregnancy and any pain you will go through as a result.

- Your husband may be freaked out about the possibility of things going wrong in the delivery room (or on the way there!). He might also be frustrated that he can't take away your pain, or scared about taking on his new role as a father.

- Your husband has fewer resources than you to draw on. You can be a powerful advocate in getting him to attend workshops, or encouraging hospitals and corporations in your area to provide workshops.

- Your husband may not feel like he's "allowed" to share his feelings with you. Subtle encouragement from you and support from other dads can help change this.

- Start sharing parenting and household duties now. Encourage your husband to participate, and encourage him to cut the baby's umbilical cord.

- If your husband has learned new parenting skills and wants to share them with you, be open to learning them.

- Be aware that your husband may be a few steps behind you in terms of adjusting, but that doesn't mean he's not catching up.

- When people and society don't acknowledge your husband as a father, this contributes to his discomfort with the role.

- Take into account that your husband is also tired, stressed, and overwhelmed after the birth, especially because he's afraid that he won't be able to provide financially.

# WE ARE AFRAID WE WON'T BE ABLE TO PROVIDE

**M**en feel financially responsible for their families. For men, the pressure to provide financially for their families runs deeper and causes more anxiety than most wives ever realize. No matter how much we earn, no matter how many hours we put in at work, no matter how hard we try, the pressure to provide *never* diminishes. This pressure is so great, in fact, that we often respond to parenthood not by caring for and bonding with a new baby, but by diving deeper into our work in pursuit of more money.

While you are struggling to care for a newborn baby, your husband may be burying himself in his work. "What on earth is wrong with my husband?" a new mom once asked me. "Instead of helping me around the house and bonding with our new baby, he's taking on more work at the office and staying there late every night!"

The truth is, your husband may be doing exactly what he feels a responsible new dad should do. Your husband's desire to be a provider may be just as strong and long-standing as your desire to be a caregiver. I remember that Tina told me she wanted to be a mother since she was five years old, and I think that most little girls have felt the same way she did. Like most little boys, I answered the "What do you want to be when you grow up?" question with things like "basketball player," "superhero," "millionaire," "cowboy," "fireman," "policeman," or "soldier." Even today, when I ask little girls what they want to be when they grow up, they often answer with "mother," but I have yet to hear any little boy answer the question with, "I want to be a father."

Your husband wants to make sure his family has the money they need, because every time money is tight, he feels ashamed. I once gave a workshop in a particularly wealthy Los Angeles suburb where most of the new and expectant dads were pretty well-off. Several of the guys were in their mid-thirties and were expecting their first babies; they owned their own homes and their own companies, and they determined their own schedules. Other guys worked in high-level management positions for well-known computer companies, law firms, and movie production companies. Were they under pressure to perform financially for their new families? You bet. Despite the fact that they were from affluent backgrounds and had a lot of stability, they clasped their white-knuckled hands and gnawed on their pens when we discussed their fears about providing. Would Greg's private company survive his two-week absence when the baby came around? Would Cole's boss let him skip the trip to China if the baby came early? Would Darren's competitive coworkers take advantage of his vulnerability as a new dad to eliminate him from the corporation? Would Wayne's law firm cut him some slack on an important legal case? Not a single dad wanted to fully confess these fears to their wives, and they wondered if their wives would understand their reluctance to leave work when they felt such a strong urge to provide.

During our conversation, there was a dad, Zach, a proud blue-collar guy working as a maintenance man for a manufacturing company, who shared a different perspective. "I worry we won't be able to pay our rent this month. I worry because we may not have the proper health insurance to cover all of the hospital bills. I worry that I haven't been working long enough to have any stability or security in my job." I sensed by the tone in his voice that he felt a little uncomfortable sharing his financial worries because he may have felt ashamed due to a lesser financial status. Though the concerns of the other men were legitimate and weighty, Zach may have wished he could trade his worries with theirs.

Fear of financial insecurity—or worse, unemployment—looms heavily on any dad's mind, and can cause him to spend more time at work than at home. As one dad put it, "Unemployment is hard on marriage. When our baby was eighteen months old, I was laid off. It took me ten months to find a job, and the only income I had was an unemployment check. We didn't have health insurance. It was a tough time for my wife and me. It really put our marriage to the test."

Remember, like I said in the last chapter, this delicate subject is like a penis-measuring contest, so if your husband is not feeling confident in this area, he's going to be *very* sensitive about it, as Zach probably was. Despite Zach's uneasiness in addressing this issue, just by attending the workshop, he was already showing his commitment to his unborn baby, no matter how young he was or what other doubts he had about his role as a provider and father.

So your husband may appear to be running away from parental responsibility, as many moms have noted. But if he's running *toward* work, step back and reevaluate the situation. Has he made little comments about the savings account lately? Has he wondered aloud if his job will be in jeopardy when he takes time off for the birth? Have you noticed him biting his fingernails while paying the bills? He may actually be taking on parental responsibility instead of running from it.

What I'm saying here builds on what I talked about in Chapter 2. Perhaps dads prepare more for the birth than meets the eye, but perhaps they do so by taking on more responsibility as providers instead of (or in addition to) caring for and bonding emotionally with the baby. In their own words, here's what dads have said about this:

> *I'm afraid if I take time off that some young buck or another employee will take over my position and/or be next in line for promotion.*

> *The issue for me is not the loss of wages or taking the time off. It's about the possibility of losing my job. Without a job, I can't provide for my family.*

> *My wife and I are struggling to make ends meet without a baby. I'm left wondering how I'm going to earn the extra money it will take to feed and clothe our baby.*

> *We're in the same boat, except I'd like to become a stay-at-home dad. I'm concerned about what it is going to be*

*like not receiving a paycheck. And how we're going to manage on one income.*

*I just received a promotion. I know this may sound selfish, but now I feel as though I will be jeopardizing a job I worked so hard to get. What am I going to tell my boss? That I can't be at work because I'm a new father? It's a scary thought.*

I'd like to emphasize that the role of provider is not a male-only domain. Obviously, I'm well aware that traditional roles are not the rule in every family, since Tina has been the breadwinner in our family for sixteen years and I've been the caretaker. Together, we've challenged a lot of the traditional roles society has prescribed for us, but it hasn't always been easy and it still results in guilt from time to time. Despite the changes occurring in our society now and the increase in the stay-at-home dad population, men feel more pressure to bring home the bacon, and it's central to their identity as men.

To illustrate how men may feel about their role as providers, let's put them side by side with some stereotypes about women as caretakers.

In workshops with dads and in workshops with moms, I have often played a word association game about mom and dad identities. On the board, I draw two columns and label one *Mom* and the other *Dad*.

"What kinds of words do you think of when you hear the word *mom?*" I ask the group. "What are some of the descriptions that come to mind? Just shout them out. There are no right or wrong answers."

"Caregiver!" someone will yell.

"Nurturer!"

"Homemaker!"

"Stressed out!"

"Good food!" somebody says with a laugh.

"Okay, good," I say, scribbling down their responses in the *Mom* column. "Now let's do the *Dad* side. What kinds of words do you think of when you hear the word *dad?*"

"Provider!"

"Disciplinarian!"

"Protector!"

"Big bad dad!"

"Goes to work!"

I write those down, too. Then I take a step back and let everybody see the results. Typically, there are about ten to twenty words in each column, depending on the size of the group I'm working with, and the columns will look something like this:

| Mom | Dad |
|---|---|
| caregiver | provider |
| nurturer | disciplinarian |
| homemaker | protector |
| stressed out | big bad dad |
| good food | goes to work |

Do you notice that the words they associate with *mom* and *dad* fall right into the gender stereotypes that haunt us all at some time or another?

That's why I play the game. I want people to see that gender stereotypes still exist. They still exist for women, and they also exist for men. When I first started doing this exercise, I was surprised to see that these stereotypes still came up, but now I realize that I shouldn't have been surprised at all, because they run deep in all our lives.

After everybody looks at the completed columns, I put a challenge to the group. "Why can't we see moms and dads working together to fulfill *all* of the positive roles you see here?" I ask, putting the marker down. "I've been a stay-at-home dad for most of my kids' lives, but people still ask my wife, 'How could you leave your kids alone with your husband?' That used to make both of us feel like bad parents. But that doesn't have to happen to you if you can get a head start at seeing these stereotypes clearly. Let's work together to give kids what they need."

I think moms understand how powerful these stereotypes are, and I want you to consider how deeply the male stereotypes influence your husband's life and view of himself. This table shows what our gender stereotypes are, how difficult they are to challenge, and how binding they can be—just like female stereotypes.

## Society Says That Working Outside the Home Is a Man's Duty

That's the stereotype in a nutshell: Dad's role is to go to work every day, whether he does it in a suit and tie or a jumpsuit with his name stitched on the patch. How I wish that stay-at-home dads could be seriously portrayed in the media as successful men, not as bumbling boobs on sitcoms who make diapers out of duct tape and paper towels and who burn macaroni and cheese! (We'll get back to the Bumbling Dad in Chapter 7). Even as a longtime caregiver, I still have to find ways to measure my success as a person that don't include being a provider, and it's difficult to this day. I have to create my own yardstick to measure success and build up my self-esteem when I don't make money for my family. Friends would come up to me and say, "You really gave up your business to stay home with the kids and let your wife be the breadwinner? How could you make such a sacrifice?" The implication was that I was crazy, lazy, selfish, or not manly. Several friends even suggested that we place our kids in day care, as if that were a better choice than having me stay at home!

Men are usually portrayed as successful in our society only when they have a nine-to-five job that rewards them with a hefty paycheck. The two most admired professional careers in our country—those of doctors and lawyers—are jobs that put a lot of stress on families. Doctors, lawyers, and other professionals are often expected to work late (or overnight), to entertain colleagues or clients at home, and, in short, to live a lifestyle that matches the job, rather than the other way around. In fact, in many cases, an "exciting" career may be one which gives you access to these lifestyles.

Speaking of exciting careers, I often see profiles in magazines or on TV of "The Top 10 Coolest Jobs Ever," which usually involve a great deal of travel. Some of the jobs I've seen profiled are travel writers, professional athletes (and their doctors), fashion photographers, and archaeologists. How amazing it would be to have a career that paid well, stimulated you intellectually, surrounded you by cool people, took you to exotic locations, and . . . let you go home to your family at five o'clock every night!

But whether his job takes him to the ends of the earth or simply chains him to his computer late night after late night, a career is a career, and it is expected that your husband be dedicated to it. He can't afford, literally and figuratively, to look like he's slacking. Even if your husband works in a blue-collar environment and thinks the word "career" is laughable, he is still expected to go the extra mile for his job. In short, what I'm saying is that most of your husband's coworkers, competitors, bosses, and clients implicitly threaten to replace him with someone more committed if they suspect he's less than dedicated to his work.

Yes, it is all of society that pushes a man to perform as a provider (and hence, as a worker, unless he was born into an inheritance of millions). It is his boss, his customers, his clients, his coworkers, and his competitors, as I said above. It's also the TV shows he's watched his entire life, it's the magazines he reads, it's the culture he's grown up in and the way he was formed in it as a child. It's his family, his relationship with you, his relationship with his kids. It's his conscience.

And that means that if he is supposed to get off at five o'clock, he may often choose to stay until six. It means that he will willingly attend evening events and dinner meetings, if he thinks they will pay off in the long run. It means he will answer his cell phone while you are trying to talk to him about the baby. It means he will work at the store on Saturday, and Sunday, too. It means he will check his e-mail again and again and again. Dads have told me a lot about how they feel on this subject.

*Balancing my job and family isn't an issue. It's whether or not my company will accept the balancing act I propose.*

*I work out of our home. I'm concerned that my wife won't be able to understand that there will be times when I can't be interrupted to help her with our baby.*

*My company offers me the choice to take advantage of the Family Medical Leave Act. But although this legislative act is designed to secure my position, I'm afraid if I do that my boss will look at me differently.*

What can you do to help? How can you help him bond with the kids and take a rest from work so the two of you can parent as a team? How can you ease the stress he feels to perform as a provider? In the next section, you'll find out about a few things you can do to ease some of the stress for him, but it is unlikely you will relieve all of it.

## How to Ease the Fear That He Won't Be Able to Provide

> Hogan's Slogan #91: "Lucky is the parent who can strip away all material possessions and be content and happy with what's left: the marriage and children."

I always say, take away all your material possessions—your house, cars, jewelry, paintings, clothes—and evaluate what you have left. If you are happy with what you see, then you're a lucky person.

That happiness is not defined by material possessions is hardly an original thought, but it is so easy to forget this in our fast-paced world that I want to highlight it. If you believe in Slogan #91, you can help relieve some of your husband's stress by talking with him about your family's

lifestyle and evaluating whether all of the material possessions he is working for are really necessary.

In some families, dad's role as provider can become
really extreme, and this can leave dads feeling resentful and
in need of support from you:

> *I want my wife and other people to view my contribution*
> *as a father as more than just a walking bank account. I*
> *think our kids benefit from a lot of things I do that go*
> *unnoticed.*

Does that sound familiar? A lot of moms say almost the
same thing this dad said! Just replace the word *father* with
*mother* and *walking bank account* with *personal maid,* and you
will see how this feeling of resentment parallels the resentment moms often have about their traditional role as caretaker.

> *I have a nice job right now. Good money but long hours.*
> *I could make a career change, but that means a cut in*
> *pay. I'm not sure my wife can live with that. She is so*
> *accustomed to a lifestyle that we can't afford if I take on*
> *a different career.*

> *When Meredith received news that she was pregnant,*
> *she not only went into nesting mode, she also went on an*
> *uncontrollable spending spree. Nothing but the best for*
> *our child. In the process, she maxed out our credit card,*
> *spending money we didn't have.*

> *I'm concerned about my wife's spending habits. Her*
> *nesting period has been costly and tapping into our sav-*
> *ings account. She feels this need to buy all this stuff I*
> *don't even think we need. Makes me wonder how my*

*parents survived without all these new gadgets they have today.*

*My wife has bought all these clothes for our child. When is the baby going to have time to wear all these clothes? I was told that all a baby does the first few months is poop, eat, and sleep.*

*The whole nesting thing has turned into a contest my wife is having with one of her friends who is also pregnant. It's like the two of them are trying to outdo each other.*

You can relieve some of your husband's stress by learning about feelings like this and offering to make some lifestyle changes. What kinds of changes are easiest to make? Here are a few ideas.

- Don't play "keeping up with the Joneses."
- Offer to create a family budget and stick to it. Hold your husband accountable, too, because dads can also fall into the "keeping up with the Joneses" trap.
- Don't use the credit card.
- Be realistic in your preparation for the baby—only buy what you can afford, and wait until after the baby shower to shop so that you know what you still need. Because babies grow so fast they hardly use their clothes, infant clothes in secondhand stores can be very nice at half the price.
- Realize that as a mom, you're bombarded with advertisements, marketing, and promotion for baby products that most people, including your husband, don't see. Be wise to the advertising: take a step back and evaluate

whether you really need the products that keep popping up in front of you like carnival clowns.

---

 AND A MOM WANTS YOU TO KNOW

## Baby Showers

Historically, baby showers have served to help new parents not only celebrate the arrival of the baby, but also to prepare for the baby's material needs. A baby shower is an event that provides new families with blankets, diapers, clothes, and so forth precisely because, in most cases, the expense of these items all at once is just too much for a young family.

So, the families and friends of the young couple get together and say, "Okay everybody, how can each of us contribute a little something so that the new baby has what it needs in order to be fed, clothed, cleaned, and cared for?" And in response, each person gives a little bit. The sum of a little bit from each person equals just about what the family needs. Pretty effective system, isn't it?

The arrival of new babies to a family requires huge amounts of energy on the part of the parents *and* the other members of the "tribe," if you will. As an anthropologist friend who studied in Africa put it, "Humans have a short interbirth interval. If we didn't live in a society with grocery stores, it would be physically impossible for a single woman to collect enough calories to support the extra caloric needs of pregnancy and lactation in addition to the caloric needs of her offspring that are not nutritionally independent. It's never just a mom and a dad supporting their offspring, it's the whole tribe." Translated to regular English, this means that babies can't survive until adulthood without the help and energy of *lots* of adults around them.

Hence the baby shower, one of the methods we use to pitch in and help provide for new babies.

Hogan said in his list above that it's a good idea to wait until after the baby shower to do shopping on your own. This is an effective way to make your money go farther, resist the temptation for a shopping blitz, and allow others to contribute, which they're usually happy to do at an exciting time like this. You can take advantage of a baby shower to reduce the "providing" burden that will fall on your and your husband's shoulders by asking your relatives and friends to chip in together on the big-ticket items like strollers, car seats, furniture, or maid service for a year.

---

I know a lot of families who have buried and overloaded their kids in a multitude of extra-curricular activities, which is stressful for moms, as we'll see in Chapter 8. Serving as chauffeur and personal organizer to kids who go to piano lessons, soccer practice, and Girl Scouts is a huge source of stress for the moms who play after-school taxi. But it's also stressful for dads, because all of the activities cost money. In addition to the cost of the activity, there's the cost of equipment, uniforms, gas, snacks, wear and tear on the car, and on and on.

Most moms don't realize how much of an impact their spending habits can have on a dad or that relieving financial stress by following a budget can actually encourage a dad to become a more involved father. The less a dad has to worry about money, the more time he'll spend at home. Think of it this way: each dollar you spend means less time for dad to be with his child; each dollar you save means more time for dad to be with his family.

Because I live in Orange County, California, I know many moms who purchase Disneyland passes. A mom named Annie confided in me about an argument she'd had with her husband after she took the kids to Disneyland.

"He asked me how come the trip to Disneyland cost us almost seven hundred dollars and said that it was outrageous and way over budget; he said that the trip was only supposed to cost two hundred. But I explained that I bought the annual pass so that we could actually save money in the long run. 'What are you talking about?' he asked. I told him, 'It costs about fifty bucks for the kids to get into Disneyland for one day, and about sixty bucks for me. But if you buy the pass, you only have to go to Disneyland three times for it to pay off, and then you can go the rest of the year for free.' He threw up his hands and walked off, as usual."

I and the other moms in the group listened to Annie, but I didn't get into the middle of the discussion. There was no way I was going to get mixed up in that argument! I just let her talk and vent her frustration at being unable to communicate with her husband about finances. What I wanted to help with in that case is getting her feelings out to reduce some of the tension she felt. Here in the book, however, you get to understand what Annie's husband was going through without having to fight with your husband to do so.

Annie's is a familiar situation in Southern California families, and, I'm sure, other places where there are great things for kids to see and do. Dads' responses to situations like Annie's, whether they say so to their wives, to me, or to no one at all, is, "Yeah, but you still spent an extra five hundred bucks of disposable income! And it's not free to keep going to Disneyland after you buy the pass! What about the gas, the wear and tear on the car, the food, the parking, and the souvenirs you have to pay for? And who said we were going to be going to Disneyland more than three times a year, anyway? All these things add up to big bucks!"

And big bucks add up to more financial obligations for dads. Here are two dads' ironic stories:

*Shari wanted me to be home more often. So I cut back on my work schedule. But at the end of each month the balance on our Visa bill either stayed the same or increased. Then Shari started complaining about our finances. The message I got was that I needed to make more money, not spend more time at home. So I went back to my regular work schedule and started working overtime. Then, Shari started complaining about me not spending more time at home. This was a confusing time for me.*

*Julia kept pressuring me to spend more time at home with the family. I wanted to, but at the end of each month I saw that the balance on the credit card bill hadn't changed much. The message I got was that I needed to work harder and make more money.*

So if you would like your husband to be more involved with the kids, take a step back and think about what you are willing to give up in return for it. The pass to the amusement park? The karate lessons? Would you even be willing to sell the house and buy a smaller one instead, or one in a city where real estate is cheaper?

When Tina and I first got married, we were both working and bought a house we could afford based on two salaries. As a working father and a provider, I felt great about that! I set my sights on an even bigger house, or one closer to the beach, and prepared to take a step up.

But then I realized our family would be taking the road less traveled. Our kids needed a parent at home, and that meant one of us would quit work, and we'd no longer be able to afford the house we already had, let alone a more expensive one. We sold our brand-new house in an upscale suburban area and moved to an area with older homes that was closer to Tina's work, cutting our mortgage and tax payments in half. We sold one of the cars, and Tina either walked to work so I could have the car, or she drove to work and I walked to the grocery store.

We cut down our expenses because we decided that the quality of our life as a family was more important than the quality of our family's lifestyle. This was a difficult decision to make in a society that measures success by how far you climb up the ladder. Money issues can be solved later, but you can't make up for lost time with your kids.

Moving was a tough decision, and it's not the right choice for everybody, but there are many ways to cut back on family expenses to ease financial tension. Each family chooses a different lifestyle based on many factors, including whether you are also working, your family's needs, and your husband's situation at work.

## Dad's Play-by-Play: What to Know from Chapter 3

- Men feel a huge amount of pressure to provide for their families.

- Husbands feel ashamed and sensitive if the family is not doing as well financially as they would like.

- Dads may think that parental responsibility equals financial responsibility.

- Male stereotypes can be just as suffocating as female stereotypes.

- The pressure on men to provide for their families comes from all aspects of society.

- The best way to help relieve some of the stress on your husband is to be more aware of the pressure and to be financially responsible by following a budget and offering to make lifestyle changes when needed.

# WE FEEL GUILTY WHEN WE DON'T SPEND TIME WITH OUR KIDS

There's no doubt that dads love their kids. I certainly love mine. Take a look at my first book, *The Man Who Would Be Dad*, and you'll find some of the most tender moments of my life revealed. For example, when Grant was a toddler, we went outside so he could show me the stars, his small chubby fingers opening and closing so he could explain their twinkling to me as I held him in my arms. Or the time Wesley and I took our picture together inside of an arcade photo booth. Or the time Matt asked me if he could take a picture of the dark in his bedroom.

Most of the time, though, dads don't share the emotional stories that bring joy to their lives or make them cry with love or sorrow, because we've been taught to stifle our emotions. I'd be in the same boat if I hadn't come to terms with my emotions as a stay-at-home dad and father of a disabled child diagnosed with Angelman Syndrome.

The fact is, males are taught to mask, stifle, and stuff their emotions from the time they are little boys, and by the time we're full-grown, married men with kids of our own, we're so good at hiding our feelings that we hardly notice we're doing it.

What happens if a man dares to express his feelings? Like I said in Chapter 3, he's usually ignored. With boys, though, exclusion and/or name-calling is the price they must pay for being honest. Boys who show emotions are teased and called names like crybaby, sissy, wimp, or Mama's boy.

Most men never get permission to express their emotions, and they never learn how to do it. In one of the Proud Dads workshops, a dad named Cole told the group, "My wife might tell you I'm a tough cookie. That's how she'd describe me. Nothing rattles me—solid as a rock, right?" Cole made a fist and shook it, and the guys nodded as he continued.

"But the downside of that is a solid rock doesn't really have a ton of warm and fuzzy emotions." Cole looked down at his hands, which were thick and greasy from his work as a European auto mechanic. "I grew up with three brothers, and my parents barely touched lips when they gave each other the 'honey I'm home' peck at the end of the day. I really didn't feel any emotions growing up except fear. I wasn't abused; I didn't even have a particularly rough childhood. My family just didn't talk much about stuff and the consequences for breaking rules were pretty stiff. Talking out my true emotions is something I have to really work on with my wife."

"How do you work on it with your kids?" I asked.

Cole's hands were shaking, and he clasped them together to steady them. "I worry about it," he said. "I'm quick to put that serious 'Dad' look on my face and use a serious tone of voice to boot so my kids instantly know I mean business. So they get my drift. But do they ever truly get that I'm there for them, to comfort them and really love them like a parent should? Do they feel warm and safe in my arms? I worry that my kids won't be able to really discuss their feelings with me as they grow—to really let it all out."

Whoa! What a burden Cole lifted off his chest in that session! I'm surprised he could speak so honestly, even if he was shaking with the effort of it. He really hadn't learned to express himself as a child and I could imagine the tough discussions he and his wife had had about honesty over the years. For some men, this is as close as they can ever come to being emotional.

A few men, though, might venture to say mushier things about parenthood:

*I believe that being involved in my daughter's life will give her the confidence she needs to select a good man who will treat her with the respect she deserves.*

*When I have a bad day, I take a moment to spend time with my daughter. I'll sit on the porch and either watch her play by herself or with other friends. Watching them gives me unparalleled joy. They provide me with a pick-me-up when I'm in the dumps. They remind me that life is good and that I should smile more.*

*Recently someone in a professional setting asked me to tell them about myself, and I answered starting with, "I'm a dad."*

*I just want to protect my kids and never let them out of my sight, but I know I have to nurture and help them find independence so they can grow into adults.*

*My wife doesn't know this, but sometimes I wake up in the middle of the night and check to see if my son is still breathing.*

*I'm afraid that I'll die before my children are fully grown, with lessons left to teach them. I'd like to teach them what it means to live in a genuine and loving relationship with God. I'm also afraid I won't be there for their big events: graduation, wedding, grandchildren, etc.*

Not giving men permission to share how they really feel has also created a bigger problem: it's hindered their ability to appreciate the precious moments they do spend with their child. By precious moments, I don't mean ones like a son or daughter hitting a home run in a baseball game, receiving an A on a report card, sinking a shot to win a basketball game, or receiving a trophy. No, I'm talking about the precious moments that don't make front page news, like the stories I mentioned at the beginning of this chapter, or private "guy stuff" like the time Grant and I were using urinals at a restaurant and Grant said, "Boy dad, we sure are looking good, aren't we?" That was one of the proudest days and father-and-son moments of my life as a dad . . . and the one that gets a lot of laughs from the dads when I tell them the story!

During the early days of my open discussion groups I came up with the idea of closing our session by asking the dads to share a funny or enlightening story about a moment they had with their child. My reasons for conducting the exercise were to end the session on a positive note and to help the fathers feel good about themselves. "Can anybody share a funny or enlightening story about something that happened to them with their child?" I asked. Silence and blank stares were all the answer I got. I waited and waited. Nobody spoke.

I was baffled.

And then the explanations dawned on me. First, most of the dads never spent enough time with their child to experience many of these moments, and if they did their minds were not on the moment but on work or other responsibilities, and the few who did spend time with their kids were caught off guard and couldn't remember. Second, most fathers don't train their minds to recognize or remember precious moments spent with their children. Third, a father may feel embarrassed to share a story or feel uneasy about delving into an emotional conversation that's out of his comfort zone, especially in a room full of strangers he thinks are too macho to understand and accept his story (even though in reality they feel the same way). So he clams up.

Instead of surrendering this exercise, I decided to find a way to make it work and help the fathers feel comfortable about participating. I came up with the following strategies:

1.  At the beginning of the session during introduction I announced my intention to have the dads share a funny or enlightening story. This gave them time to tap into their memory bank.
2.  I shared two or three of my own stories as examples of what I was looking for.
3.  I talked with the dads before the session started to learn

more about them and find some way of getting them to tell me a funny story about their child. Then I would invite one of those guys to be the first to share the story at the end of the session.

The results exceeded my expectations. In one workshop attended by 110 dads, the guys formed a line near the stage and couldn't wait to get in front of the microphone. The line got so long that I had to give the dads extra time to tell their stories. Unfortunately, due to time constraints I had to put an end to the bragging session and send the dads back to their chairs!

This exercise demonstrates that when given the proper direction, instruction, and opportunity a man can and will answer the call to emotionally connecting with his child, which in turn leads him to become a more caring, involved husband and father. But this can't happen unless we all first remove the stereotyping and mental barriers we have of men as fathers that I mentioned in the previous chapter.

Dads do love their kids. So how do they feel about leaving when they go off to work every morning (or afternoon, or evening) to fulfill their provider role? Let me explain.

## Working Dad, Working Mom: Same Guilt

Whenever I'm surfing the Web, reading parenting books, or talking to moms, I hear a lot about the guilt that working moms feel about leaving their kids when they go off to work. Moms from my workshops have said they feel guilty when they can't keep up the rigorous pace and unrealistic expectations they often set for themselves. Some moms feel guilty because they can't chaperone school field trips, have to miss out on gymnastics meets, and don't have time to help their child with math homework. One mom even shared that she felt guilty leaving the baby alone with her husband. "Why?" I asked. She told me that if something happened to the baby while under her husband's watch, she wouldn't blame her husband, she would blame *herself* for not being there to protect the child from getting hurt!

I think some of the toughest days for Tina were the times she had to go to work when one of the boys was sick. I could see the guilt and anguish on her face and the "I'm a bad mother for not being there for my child" look as she left the house to go to work. This was especially true when it came to Wesley, who was constantly in and out of the hospital, and frequently had to visit the doctor or attend therapy sessions.

But what was even more painful for Tina was missing out on many "first-time moments" I had the privilege of witnessing. Although I would tell her about them, it didn't ease the pain of not being there to bask in the excitement of witnessing them firsthand. Try to imagine and be sympathetic to how your husband must feel when he comes home and receives secondhand news about an exciting moment you had with the child. It would be like missing out on a movie you really wanted to see and having your friend tell you, "That's okay. I'll just tell you what happened instead." Not quite the same experience, is it?

Another group of people who experience this guilt are dads.

That's right, the guilt that moms feel when balancing work and kids happens to dads, too. Working dads, like working moms, can feel just as much anguish when they miss out on important events or even day-to-day activities with their kids. Most of the time dads don't speak up because they've been taught not to show emotion or because they've been so completely excluded from the nurturer role that they don't feel it's their place to ask for a share in it.

*I want to work in order to provide financial security for my family and children's future. But I also don't want to miss out on spending time with them.*

*I do a lot of traveling. I'm concerned about how I'll be able to stay connected and bond with our child. But more importantly, how am I going to deal with explaining to him why I couldn't be there to watch his baseball game?*

In 1999, I participated in an ABC *Fathers and Sons* television documentary with our disabled son, Wesley. One of the other guys in the documentary was a dad who was a fisherman. I'm not talking about somebody who got up early on Saturdays and put on a goofy hat with fishhooks in it to smoke stogies and swat mosquitoes in an aluminum boat with his buddies, but a real-life professional fisherman who worked on a big fishing boat off the coast. His boat trips lasted several weeks *each*.

Talk about guilt! This guy felt horrible about leaving his son for days and weeks at a time and worried that he couldn't be there for him. With a breaking voice, he related how his own father was never around to watch his sporting events because he was just too busy. "And the sad thing about it is that I'm doing the same thing to my kids," he added. You could tell by watching him that he and his son really missed each other when they were apart.

I know a lot of fathers who are firefighters, military service personnel, police officers, sales reps, and doctors feel the same way when their jobs take them far from home, often against their wishes. Remember, these professions provide valuable services and products for other parents and their children. Like the fisherman, these dads can be too hard on themselves, and so can the people around them.

To help me stay in the mindset of team parenting despite all the challenges of balancing work and family, I like to remember this:

**Hogan's Slogan # 37: "Parents are not two people filling two roles, but two people filling one role."**

I see parenthood as a team effort in which the nurturing and providing both come into play. How each family divides up the tasks between two people varies depending on the situation. No matter how you and your husband are balancing things, one or both of you is likely to feel guilty if you see yourselves as falling short of your ideal, and no one enjoys feeling guilty. To assuage some of your own guilt, read Chapter 8. To help your husband with his, try some of these tips:

- If your kids are young and waking up for school is not an issue, move bedtime to a later hour so Dad has more quality time in the evening with them. Then let the kids sleep in the next morning.
- Remind your children to show age-appropriate gratitude to whoever works for the things the paychecks buy them. Teach them to say, "Thank you, Dad," and "Thank you, Mom," when they get new shoes or a trip to the water park. They need to know that new shoes don't pay for themselves.

- Instead of using vacation time to take a trip, consider staying home and using it to be more involved with the kids. Let Dad ferry them to their usual activities or camp out in the backyard with them. Or, spread vacation days out over the year so you don't miss as many crucial activities.
- When Dad comes home and the kids make a beeline for him, step back and let them play rough.
- Get his input on household rules, chores, and other issues.
- Maintain family get-together times, like dinner on certain days of the month, and hold your kids to the schedule even if they're in high school and think it's corny.

Dads are doing what they can to balance providing and nurturing. Part of the problem is that they don't have enough time to do both (just like working moms) and the other part is that they may see their role as nurturer as being very small.

## Dads Have Less Time to Learn to Parent

Dads have less time to learn to parent if they've spent less time with their kids. As we'll see in Chapter 6, dads don't want you to teach them parenting skills any more than they want to ask directions if they get lost while driving (but you have probably figured this out already if you've tried to teach your husband how to put a sippy cup together correctly and gotten a lot of eye-rolling in response). Guys prefer to save face and figure it out on their own.

What happens when he only spends six hours per week with the kids, and you spend sixty-plus hours, or thirty if you're a working mom? The consequence is that he can't learn to parent as quickly as you because he doesn't have enough time to practice. Dads will appear to be light-years behind mom not only emotionally, as we saw in Chapter 2, but also in terms of parenting skills. Dad can't seem to find the diaper rash ointment? Maybe he hasn't ever used it. Dad forgot to pack a juice box with his daughter's lunch? Maybe he's not in the habit of it.

This is not to say you should feel sorry for your husband or bail him out—no way! I just want you to see why he is a step behind you and what's causing your frustration. Tina works with the schools, and one thing I've learned from hanging around teachers is this old saying:

*"Tell me and I'll forget.*
*Show me and I might remember.*
*Involve me and I'll understand."*

In keeping with this great idiom of education, I say,

Hogan's Slogan #62:
"Nag him and he'll forget on purpose.
Show him and he'll roll his eyes.
Let him do it and he'll do it proudly."

---

## ♀AND A MOM WANTS YOU TO KNOW

### Where to Draw the Line and How to Solve the Conflict That Could Ensue

Okay, so dads don't have as much time to learn parenting skills, and they appear helpless because they can't find the diaper ointment and forget to pack the juice box. In most cases, I think that's an honest predicament. But what if it's not?

As kids, my sister and I thought this Shel Silverstein poem was hilarious:

> If you have to dry the dishes
> (Such an awful, boring chore)
> If you have to dry the dishes
> ('Stead of going to the store)
> If you have to dry the dishes
> And you drop one on the floor—
> Maybe they won't let you
> Dry the dishes anymore.

(From *A Light in the Attic.* New York: HarperCollins, 1981.)

Har, har. It was funny when I was eight, but it wouldn't be funny if my husband were reciting it today. If your husband is playing the "helpless guy" card to get out of household or childcare duties, here's what I recommend: don't fall for it. And don't let your kids pick up this habit, either.

Ann Landers used to say that nobody can take advantage of you without your permission. If you are being treated like the servant of the house, it is time for you to stop serving. If someone asks you where the milk is, say, "I'm not going to answer silly questions like that. You're a smart guy (or a smart kid) and you can probably find it yourself." Do not, under any circumstances, play into this game by going to the kitchen, opening the refrigerator, and getting out the milk.

If your husband yells at you from two rooms away, "Honey! What day is it today?" do not, do not, do not drop what you are doing, walk over to your husband, and consult the calendar right above his head for him. Just yell back, "There's a calendar above your head!"

If your kids leave their clothes in a pile on the bathroom floor and you are sick of telling them to pick them up and take them to the hamper, just stop telling them. They will learn to pick up their clothes when they find out that their uniform or their favorite jeans are not clean and they'll have to wear them dirty. A pile of clothes on the floor for a week is a small price to pay to save your vocal cords and your dignity.

If someone tries to guilt-trip you or blame you for a messy house, or for being grumpy or a bad mother, you can say this: "I'm not your servant. You're capable of doing that yourself." Then walk away and don't feel guilty. Otherwise, you are training everybody in your house that using you is okay, and it's not.

---

Dads have less time to learn to parent if they work full time and also because they may have missed out on nurturing role modeling as kids. In the next chapter, we'll dig deep into your husband's past to explore this topic.

## Dad's Play-by-Play: What to Know from Chapter 4

- Dads love their kids, but have a hard time expressing tender feelings.

- Like working moms, working dads feel guilty when they can't be there for their kids.

- Parenthood is *one* role filled by *two* people, not *two* roles for *two* people.

- If possible, make more time for your husband to spend with the kids.

- Dads have less time to learn to parent than moms, so they may appear inept.

- ... but if you think he's playing a passive-aggressive "helpless dad" game, don't reward it by waiting on him or the kids.

- Most dads have not had as much nurturer role modeling as moms have had.

# WE ARE DEEPLY AFFECTED BY OUR OWN FATHERS

The role your husband's dad played (or didn't play) in his life deeply affects his approach to fatherhood. That doesn't mean if he had a negative experience that he'll necessarily reproduce it, because many dads do just the opposite. In fact, today's dads are challenging and changing the concept of fatherhood every day. What it does mean is that his childhood and teenage experience with his dad are a big part of his concept of fatherhood.

In my workshops, I ask guys to talk about their dads. "Now let's talk about your own fathers," I said to a group of men at a father's event in Los Angeles. No one jumped out of his seat with excitement, but as usual, I included this exercise in the workshop because it was important to heal any wounds they had, to help them come to terms with their fathers, and to understand how it will affect their future role as fathers and help them move forward in a positive direction. The point of the exercise is not to be judgmental, but to understand where our fathers were coming from a generation ago and how that affects us today.

In general, guys have a difficult time talking about emotional childhood experiences with many people, if any. Not because they don't want to, but because they have been conditioned not to, as I've noted in various examples throughout this book. However, through my experience in conducting these fathering workshops, I know that if given the opportunity, men are capable of discussing and sharing a variety of sensitive issues with each other. And that's a great thing for moms, because these sessions serve as a training ground for the dads to further discuss this and other important issues with their wives.

To put the group more at ease, I use myself as an example. First, I tell the men that if they feel uncomfortable talking about their fathers that they can choose to pass. Next I explain how their fathers, and their fathers before them, were only doing what they were taught to do: to bring home the bacon and leave the caregiving and household duties to moms. It was also a time when fathers weren't allowed in the labor and delivery room. I ask the dads to consider how emotionally painful it must have been for their fathers to have been excluded from witnessing the birth of their child. Then I tell the dads how fortunate they are to have a class for expectant dads available to them.

## Negative Father Figures

Finally, to help break the ice, I share my story of life without my father. "My mom and dad divorced when I was two," I begin, making a conscious effort to maintain eye contact with the dads. I always do this to make sure I get their undivided attention and show them that I am very comfortable in talking honestly about my father. Eye contact is a form of communication males use as a challenge, and it's also a call to arms. This is my way of challenging and inviting them to step up to the plate and follow my lead.

> I was born in Brazil, and my mom moved me and my brother away after the divorce and never talked to us about my dad, Henk. I never got a phone call, letter, or birthday card from him. Ever.
>
> Over the years, I gave up all hope of ever meeting my dad again. I really thought to myself, "I don't have a dad." I'll tell you, life without a father was pretty painful. My mom didn't have a lot of money, and we moved around all the time. When I say we moved around a lot, I mean we were practically nomadic! By the time I was twelve, we had lived in three different countries, eight different cities, and ten different apartments. From Brazil, we moved to Holland, and then to New Orleans, then to Los Angeles, and then in apartments all over LA County. Those apartments were in some tough, gang-infested, and impoverished neighborhoods, too. I was attacked on the street twice, once with a knife.
>
> In those rough neighborhoods and the rough schools I went to, I learned quickly that as a boy, I had to be tough. It didn't matter that I was small and skinny as a little kid, or that kids called me all kinds of racial slurs for my Asian features. I couldn't cry, hug, or talk about wish-

ing I had a dad. I didn't have a dad to teach me how to work through the teasing and stand up for myself. If someone called me a sissy and pushed me on the street after school, I had to call him a name and push him back.

The only advantage I had was my height and athletic abilities [I am six-foot-six]. I'd always been small, but in high school I really shot up, and by the time I was a senior I was six-foot-five. Sports gave me self-confidence, showed me to hold my own against other people, and taught me about competition, strategy, and teamwork in a safe environment. Plus, sports are "manly" activities, so I felt accepted by other kids. But none of that could make up for a dad, especially when I was a teenager and needed to learn about girls, sex, and planning for my future.

Then I share something that I don't want to happen to my kids: losing the direction and focus they will need to accomplish their dreams.

As it was, I didn't have much direction, and I never finished college. And because of some bad decisions I made, I lost an opportunity of becoming an NCAA and NBA basketball player.

Finally, when I was twenty-nine, my brother met someone through work who had the same last name as we did. It turned out to be our uncle Theo, my father's brother! He put us in touch with our father, and I arranged to travel to Brazil to meet him and stay with him for six months. When Henk hugged me at the airport in Curitiba (a city southwest of Rio De Janeiro), he started crying and couldn't stop. It was so strange to see this guy I had only known in a couple of pictures bawling his eyes out over me! During my stay in Curitiba, Henk told me that he had tried to contact us, but my mom and her relatives wouldn't let him. He sent us letters, but they were returned unopened. That day was the beginning of a great father-son relationship. A lot of puzzle pieces fell into place for me about my childhood and who I am. It was amazing to hear Henk's side of the story, and I went back to Brazil two more times.

What an awesome, life-changing experience it was to get to know my dad!

After a while, it dawned on me that he had missed me even more than I had missed him. The bright side of the story is that my childhood without a dad has motivated me to be a hands-on, emotionally involved father to my own kids. I want them to have a role model and a guide in life. I want them to feel safe and go to college. I want them to be good husbands and fathers. . . . Plus, I have a selfish reason for being in their lives: I never want to feel the pain that Henk felt when he wasn't a part of me and my brother's lives.

Next, I invite the dads to share their own experiences with the group. "Now it's your turn. Tell us about your dad," I said.

In all these years, only one person has ever passed on this. There are other men who share stories like mine, about not having had a father at all. There's no doubt it's painful, but I can't help thinking that it could be a whole lot worse.

I've heard some really emotional stories from guys whose dads were at home but whose presence in the family was negative. There are some guys who have told me about fathers who were emotionally and physically abusive. Other guys have told me how they were baffled by fathers who inhabited the house but were completely detached from their kids and never got involved in parenting unless major discipline was in order. Uninvolved dads were pretty common in the past: after all, we're talking about a generation of fathers who weren't even allowed in the delivery room to witness the greatest miracle in life—the birth of their own child.

It's amazing to watch these men go through this powerful and enlightening exercise, and I've been witness to many moving moments. How and what the dads share about their fathers has certainly dispelled many of the unfortunate myths that have been made about men.

For the most part, today's dads want to be involved with their families and struggle to conquer any negative images of fatherhood that they have. Here is what they say about negative father images:

*My father was an alcoholic and a real son-of-a-bitch. Hardnosed, tough guy, wouldn't give me an inch. If I got out of line, I'd get a whipping from his belt. I was afraid of my father. I don't want my child to be afraid of me.*

*I love my father, but he was way too hard on me. He was also not around much. We hardly talked, but the thing is, he didn't know any better. His father wasn't around for him. So I guess he figured he didn't need to be around for me. I'm here today because I don't want to follow in my grandfather's or my father's footsteps.*

*My dad left when I was four years old. He was an alcoholic and drug addict. Don't know where he is. He's probably in some jail. I care and I don't care. But if I did ever meet up with him, I do have one question for him: why were alcohol and drugs more important than me?*

*My dad was around, but not very hands-on. He relied a lot on Mom to do most of the work. He was one of the couch-potato dads. He'd come home, eat, watch TV, and go to bed. I used to be upset at him. Now I feel sorry for him because he missed out on so much. I've probably spent more time with my three-year-old son than my dad spent with me in the first eighteen years of my life.*

A guy who wants to be involved with his kids when his own dad was absent, abusive, or uninvolved deserves high praise and encouragement from the people who love him and from society in general. (This is a lot like women who climb corporate ladders deserving our respect and admiration for challenging their stereotypes.) After all, it's very difficult to know how to behave, what to say, and how to create a new concept of yourself when you're out of your element like this.

If your husband is bravely getting involved in the messy, emotional, topsy-turvy world of parenting, reward his behavior and you'll probably get more of it. When he gets involved with his kids, here are some ways to encourage him:

- Thank him and be specific about the time he spent and what he did with the child. You can say things like, "Honey, that was really neat the way you handled Devon's temper tantrum," or "Kristy told me how much fun she had playing house with you this afternoon."
- Teach your kids how to thank and compliment their dad.
- Ask friends and family to acknowledge your husband's contribution.

- Get the kids excited when he comes home from work or is going to spend time with them on his own. "Hey, you guys! I hear Dad coming home!" and "Guess what? Daddy's taking you to the park tomorrow! Yay!" are some things that work.
- Listen when your husband talks about his own childhood because you may be the only person he's ever talked to about it.

## Positive Father Figures

In contrast to the last section, lots of dads who come to Proud Dads workshops have had wonderful fathers. If your husband had a great father who was an emotionally and physically involved dad a generation ago, he's one lucky guy. Keep in mind that he may have some feelings of pressure and perfectionism about living up to that standard.

> Hogan's Slogan #88: "There is no such
> thing as a perfect dad."

Help your husband realize that he will not and cannot be a perfect father, and that's okay. Here's what guys have said about living up to the image of their fathers:

*I can't say enough good things about my dad. He was awesome. He was a hard worker, but he always found a way to make time for me. And when he couldn't, he'd always talk to me and explain why. He had a tough job. He was a police officer. And there were times when he just couldn't be around because he was helping other people and making the world safe for me and my mom. I've got some big shoes to fill.*

*My dad wasn't only a great father, he was a great hus-*
*band. Yeah, he and my mom had their disagreements*
*and challenges, but he treated my mom with the utmost*
*respect. It's going to be hard, but I want to be just like*
*him.*

There are only so many hours in the day, as moms know
all too well. A dad who is involved with his kids, does housework, and holds down a full-time job is a blessing to his family and to society, just like moms who do the same.

There have been men who bring their own fathers to my
workshops, and this is a very moving experience. One
expectant father said, "This is an important moment in my
life. I thought, why not share it with my best friend? So I
brought my dad."

The older dads have had some interesting insights themselves on the way fatherhood has changed in the last forty
years:

*I came to this class with my son to support him. He*
*wants to be the hands-on father I wasn't for him and I*
*want to help him do that for his child. I guess you could*
*say that I'm making up for lost time by being a hands-on*
*grandfather.*

*I think I was a pretty good father. . . . Right, son? But I*
*didn't change diapers, bathe, or dress our kids. That was*
*his mother's job. My job was to earn the money. I think*
*it's great that you guys have this class. I wish I had had*
*it. I think I would have been a much better dad.*

*I haven't said much today because I'm here as more of a*
*companion for my son. This is kind of a culture shock*

*for me, sitting with a bunch of guys listening to you talk about, you know . . . this fatherhood, sex, and raising kids stuff. It wasn't our cup of tea back in my day. I thought this was going to be one of those touchy-feely things, but it's not. As I look around, I see how valuable this class will be for my son. I think all you guys are very lucky to have a class like this available. All of you are going to be much better prepared to be a father than I ever was.*

*I tell you what, times sure have changed since I was a father. We never had a class like this and I'm not sure I would have attended one. But after listening to you guys, I realize this is a good thing. I also see how much I missed out on. I hope I can make up for lost time by helping my son care for his child in the way I didn't do it for him. I never changed a diaper. It will be neat to have my son teach me how to do it with my grandchild. I guess I'll be more hands-on as a grandfather than I ever was as a father.*

*My relationship with my son hasn't been all that great. But things between us have changed for the better since he told me he was going to be a father. That meant I was going to be a grandfather! When he invited me, I wasn't sure I wanted to go. But then I realized that by inviting me he was telling me that regardless of all my shortcomings, he still loves me. So here I am.*

I am really grateful to the expectant dads and grandfathers who had the courage to attend the workshops together and who were able to share their feelings with the group. They're some of the bravest guys I've ever met.

In my work, I meet lots of brave guys who have really changed the way fathers are seen in this day and age. Dads like Elliott, who's not afraid to kiss and hug his kids in public. Dads like Ben, who mops floors, changes diapers, and does laundry. Or like Carlos, who volunteers at his kids' elementary school and visits them for lunch. Or J.P., who leads a dads' playgroup. In my mind, marching to the beat of a different drum is really brave.

## The Father-in-Law

Your own concept of fatherhood will also impact your husband's experience as a father.[†] Why is that? Because you use your concept of fatherhood as a yardstick to measure your husband's performance. Your concept of fatherhood is based in large part on what kind of father you had. There are three primary ways your concept of fatherhood will impact your perception of your husband:

- If your father was controlling or abusive, you may have come to perceive his behavior as normal during your childhood. If you lived with abuse or tension every day of your childhood, you may have gotten used to that conflict as a normal state of dynamics in your family. If so, you may be unconsciously uncomfortable when your own husband takes on too much of an emotional or nurturing role in your family. You may even find his behavior as a nurturer "unmanly" if it goes against your concepts of what a man should do.

---

[†]Your father figure may have been a stepfather, grandfather, or combination of all three. If so, that is perfectly okay and you can use whichever man (or men) you feel appropriate as the father figure for the exercises in this chapter.

- If your father was controlling or abusive and you are try-ing to make your adult life the polar opposite of your childhood, you may judge your husband's behavior in terms of how *different* he is from your father. Conflict could arise if you perceive his behaviors as being too close to the abusive, controlling father figure you are try-ing to leave behind.

- If you had an amazing father and want your husband to be just like him, you are a lucky woman indeed, but there is one place to watch for conflict: you are destined to view your husband as a failure if you want him to be just like your dad, because he's a different person. Nobody can exactly replicate someone else's life because no two lives are the same. I think it's easier to under-stand this if the roles are reversed—how disgusted would you feel if your husband compared you to his own mother? Especially because of the cultural shifts we've seen in the last two generations, it would be annoying to have your husband compare you to his mom all the time. If you're working and your mother-in-law didn't work outside of the home, imagine having to hear from your husband, "Well, *my* mom made homemade cookies every Thursday and mended all of our clothes by hand and never needed a cleaning lady!" That wouldn't be fair to you.

These three concepts of fatherhood aren't mutually exclusive; you may have had a father who was a very posi-tive force in some areas of your life, but who was domineer-ing in others. Or, if your father was abusive, you may consciously want to break free from this concept of father-hood, but subconsciously be so used to it that it has become a "comfort zone" for you.† In the end, you, like your husband, have a concept in your mind of what a father is and what a father should be. Your values, experience, culture, childhood, and goals all contribute to your understanding of fatherhood, for better or for worse. Your concept of fatherhood influences how you evaluate your husband's behavior as a father and whether your family life is satisfying to you.

Below is a short, fun exercise to help you reveal some of the ways in which your perception of your own father can influence your perception of your husband. This exercise is not intended to be a substitute for therapy, but simply something to get your mind going.

### Step-by-Step Evaluation of Your Father Concept

For questions one through four, rate on a scale of 1–5, with 1 being excellent and 5 being poor.

1.  Rate your satisfaction with your husband as a husband.

    1    2    3    4    5

2.  Rate your satisfaction with your husband as a father.

    1    2    3    4    5

3.  Rate your satisfaction with your father as a father.

    1    2    3    4    5

4.  Rate your impression of who your father was as a husband to your mother (or stepmother).

    1    2    3    4    5

---

† If your father was abusive or controlling, you may benefit from a few sessions of professional counseling.

5. As husbands, how similar do you think these two men are?

   Very similar—they could be clones
   Somewhat similar
   Neutral
   Different
   Very different—they are like night and day

6. As fathers, how similar do you think these two men are?

   Very similar—they could be clones
   Somewhat similar
   Neutral
   Different
   Very different—they are like night and day

7. What first attracted you to your husband?

8. Which of your husband's attributes convinced you that he was the one to marry?

9. What do you love about your father?

10. What do you dislike about your father?

11. What frustrates you most about your marriage?

12. What do you fight about most with your husband?

13. What do you think is the biggest difference between your husband's concept of fatherhood and your own concept of fatherhood?

Do you see a pattern emerging? You might find that there are clusters of behaviors that your father and husband have in common. You might find there are others in which they are polarized. Each of these two men operates with a different set of circumstances in life, not the least of which is the time period he became a father in. The purpose of this exercise is to bring light to your concept of fatherhood and how you perceive your husband's behavior so that you can minimize conflict in your marriage.

I don't think you should view your husband's situation as a reason to let him off the hook when it comes to being an involved dad—not at all. Don't say to yourself, "My own dad was amazing and my husband will never live up to that, so I might as well forget about asking him to take the kids to soccer on Saturday." Kids absolutely need their dads in their lives! But I do think that understanding your husband's situation will help you see his behavior more clearly and can ultimately reduce conflict and fights with your husband.

---

## ♀AND A MOM WANTS YOU TO KNOW
### Reducing Conflict with Assertiveness

A friend of mine who is a licensed clinical psychologist gave me an amazingly simple description of assertive behavior that I'd like to share with you. This is a great way to ask people for what you want without starting a conflict.

Let's say you are back in high school again, sitting at a desk in math class. Your teacher says to the class, "Okay everybody, take out your notes! Let's get to work on Unit Three, quadratic equations!" Everyone groans and you all get out your books, notes, and pencils . . . except Andrew, who sits next to you—he realizes he's forgotten his pencil! While you are hard at work and listening to the teacher, Andrew is eyeing the extra one you have on the edge of your desk. He'd like to use that extra pencil himself.

Andrew has four choices about what kind of behavior he'll use to borrow your pencil. They are: passive, aggressive, passive-aggressive, and assertive. Here are the scenarios:

**Passive**: Andrew looks pointedly at your pencil. He turns his body to you, sighs, turns away again, and slumps down in his desk. He thinks to himself, *What is wrong with her? Can't she see that I don't have a pencil? Why doesn't she offer her extra pencil to me? I'm looking right at her pencil! She must be blind!* Obviously, you don't have telepathy and have no idea that Andrew would like your pencil. You keep on taking notes while Andrew continues his sighing, slumping, and thinking.

**Aggressive**: Andrew sees that you have an extra pencil, so he just grabs it without asking.

**Passive-aggressive**: Andrew looks pointedly at your pencil. He turns his body to you, sighs, turns away again, and slumps down in his desk. He thinks to himself, *What is wrong with her? Can't she see that I don't have a pencil? Why doesn't she offer her extra pencil to me? I'm looking right at her pencil! She must be blind!* Obviously, you don't have telepathy and have no idea that Andrew would like your pencil. You keep on taking notes while Andrew continues his sighing, slumping, and thinking. After a while, Andrew becomes impatient and angry. He thinks, *I'm tired of waiting for her to offer me that extra pencil! She's stingy! I've waited and suffered long enough, and now I've missed five minutes of note-taking because of her! If I get a bad grade, it'll be all her fault! I'm entitled to take that pencil after what she's put me through.* He leans over and grabs your pencil without asking.

**Assertive**: Andrew notices that you have an extra pencil. He leans over and says to you, "I forgot my pencil today. Can I please borrow yours?"

This is the simplest description I've ever heard of passive, aggressive, passive-aggressive, and assertive behaviors. Women are often accused of passive-aggressive behavior, and I know I've been guilty of it myself. I think it often happens when I feel I don't have the right to ask for what I need or want, so I have to find other ways of getting it. It also happens when we try to avoid conflict by minimizing our requests. However, passive-aggressive behavior can result in HUGE fights because nothing is ever said out loud, so communication is broken down from the get-go. Also, avoiding conflict actually *causes* conflict when you wind up frustrated because you don't have things you need.

The most effective and least conflict-inducing way to ask your husband for something is to ask for it assertively. Start with an "I" statement and follow up with a simple request, *and then stop.* Here are a few examples:

- "I have my hands full. Can you please carry the trash out on your way to the car?"
- "I don't have time to help the kids with their homework tonight. Can you please check their spelling?"
- "I have a headache and need to lie down. Can you please take care of dinner tonight?"

It can be hard to stop talking after your request and not tack on a bunch of rationalizations after you state it, à la "my headache is really, *really,* bad, and there's a Tupperware with spaghetti in the fridge and you never make dinner anyway, so this is more than fair." Stating your requests assertively takes practice ... and courage. With time, you can feel better and more confident about asking for things, and your husband will probably be less prickly if he is on the receiving end of assertive behavior instead of one of the other types. This is a great way to reduce conflict in your marriage.

---

I hope you've come into a greater understanding of who today's fathers are and what issues they're grappling with in their role as dads. You might want to review this chapter or repeat the exercise in a few days. For now, we're about to embark on the topics that moms most enjoy in Chapters 6–10! These chapters will teach you how to liberate yourself from too much work, stress, and heartache in your family life and empower you with practical, encouraging, and motivational methods to help your husband play a more involved role as a father.

## Dad's Play-by-Play: What to Know from Chapter 5

- The role your husband's father played in his life impacts his concept of himself as a father.
- Positive affirmations that your husband is a good father can help boost his self-confidence.
- It takes a great deal of courage for today's parents to take on new roles as fathers and mothers so that they can parent as a team.
- Your own concept of fatherhood impacts how you view your husband's fathering.
- Understanding fathering and using assertive behavior can greatly reduce conflict and tension in your marriage.

# WE CAN TAKE CARE OF
# BABIES AND KIDS!

Does it seem to you like your husband is not willing to help with the childcare? There may be something you can do about it . . . or *not* do!

Let me explain: Most dads are ready, willing, and able to be involved with their kids and be a part of their children's lives. Yet the dads in my workshops have confided that they often feel that their efforts in the childcare department are not appreciated by their wives, and in fact, their wives may have accidentally pushed them out of the child-rearing arena. As you'll see in Chapter 7, this is a common issue in the household chore department as well. To help your husband get the hang of childcare, first give him some time to learn and bond.

## I Need as Much Time to Learn as You Did

If you're becoming frustrated with your husband's inability to help the kids get dressed, brush their teeth, or take a bath, remember that he may still be learning the basics, especially if he works full time. Your husband needs time to learn on his own.

To illustrate this point, I asked a group of moms in one of my workshops, "How do you feel when your mom or your mother-in-law gives you advice, old-school remedies, or criticizes the way you care for your baby?"

The moms in the group were obviously fed up with such "help." I got a lot of answers:

*I hate when she does that!*

*It makes me feel incompetent.*

*It makes me feel like I'm not being a good mother.*

Unwittingly, this is how moms make their husbands feel when they try to teach parenting skills to them. Hard as it is, if you want your husband to have a happy attitude toward parenting, the most effective tactic is to bite your tongue and let him learn.

"But why does my husband take forever to learn these things?" one mom asked. "The baby's two months old, and he's still acting like he doesn't know how to change a diaper. He's a smart guy! He should be just as capable as I am."

Of course—unless he only changes a diaper a few times a week. In other words, if your husband works full time, he may only have eight or ten hours a week to devote to child care, during which he can't possibly keep up with the skills and bonding you accomplish in sixty-plus hours a week.

Even so, dads don't want to be bailed out. *Don't step in and re-diaper the baby yourself.* If you do, your husband is likely to throw up his hands and wonder why he bothered at all. Dads say they want a chance to learn from their mistakes: if they haven't put on a diaper tightly enough, they'll soon learn the consequences on their own!

Here's what dads have said on this subject:

*I wish my wife would treat me like an equal partner and not an assistant.*

*I think it would be nice if my wife would let me take care of the baby without giving me specific instructions. If something doesn't work out with the baby, I'll figure it out or call her for help.*

*Don't pack the diaper bag for me. Let me learn how to do it.*

This logic applies to understanding baby talk, learning what foods kids like, and choosing age-appropriate toys. Your husband may appear to take forever to learn these skills, but if you count up the hours spent on these activities, he may not be that much slower than you. Factor in that you may have had previous childcare experience as a teenage babysitter or as an adult trusted with the care of nieces and nephews, experiences your husband may not have had.

Getting bailed out of sticky situations, no pun intended, may be convenient for a dad at the time. But over the years, it results in resentment that gets articulated as, "My wife never lets me do anything with the kids."

"So what can we do about it?" asked Theresa, a woman at one of my workshops for moms. Theresa was particularly frustrated by her husband's seeming ineptness at childcare.

"It's not what you should do, it's what you should *not* do," I answered. "Don't pack the diaper bag for your husband. Don't leave him a list of items to put into the diaper bag. In fact, don't even remind him to take the diaper bag with him at all! He'll learn after one or two outings how to do things on his own, and you won't have to stress about being his personal assistant." When she heard this, Theresa raised her eyebrows and nodded.

This isn't to say you shouldn't communicate with your husband about your child's needs—of course you should let him know if you think the baby is going through a growth spurt and is eating like a horse so that he can bring extra milk or formula. But don't pack the bottles for him. He might have to make a stop at the drugstore if he's forgotten something, and chances are, making an extra stop will be fine with him.

---

## 🤰AND A MOM WANTS YOU TO KNOW
### Benefits of a Co-Ed Baby Shower

When I was about six months pregnant, I had a conversation I'll never forget with a friend whose two boys were in elementary school. She told me, "Let your husband get involved with the baby from the very beginning. After the baby is born, as soon as you can walk and drive, go to the grocery store by yourself. Don't leave your husband a list of things to do while you're gone. Just go. He needs to be able to do it on his own." She then told me about a friend of hers whose marriage was falling apart, largely due to the woman's inability to let the man take part in childcare, and her subsequent frustration that her husband never helped out.

I took this advice and I am forever grateful to her for being so direct with me. One example of how this has worked for us happened when we were planning the baby shower.

When we selected gifts for our registry, I passed the scanner to my husband and let him beep away, too. "Here," I said, "you choose the diaper bag."

He looked at me, aghast. "Me? I have no idea what to choose! I've never picked out a diaper bag before."

"Me, either," I said.

"Are you sure you want *me* to do this?" he asked.

"I trust you," I told him. He took several diaper bags down from the shelf, opened them, examined the bells and whistles that came with each one, put the straps over his shoulder and tested how comfortable they were to carry. He then chose a great diaper bag . . . and later was eager to use it.

I also insisted on a co-ed baby shower, which is becoming more common these days. Many kind friends and family members were excited about the arrival of our baby, and since half of them were men, I didn't feel it would be right to exclude them from this important event to welcome the baby. My husband came, and so did his male friends. We skipped the typical baby-shower games in favor of a less structured atmosphere with cake, chips, soda, and gifts. Afterwards, several of the guys thanked us for including them and said it was an amazing experience—they'd never had a chance to go to a baby shower before, and they really liked it.

These guys (and their wives and girlfriends) have continued to welcome our daughter into their lives as she grows. When we're invited to someone's house for dinner, our daughter is included, and nobody acts as if a toddler messes up the atmosphere or cramps their style (and these guys are professional musicians!). As a result, our daughter is talked to, cherished, and valued by a large group of caring men and women who provide enriching experiences and help build up her self-esteem. I can never repay my friend for her timely advice and the benefits it has brought our daughter.

## Please Let Go So I Can Bond

Another reason to give your husband time with the kids is the important chance you give them to bond with each other. In fact, after your husband has been at work all day, the kids may be hungry for his attention and could even misbehave in front of him if they're not getting it.

The bonding is good for the kids, it's good for your husband, and it's good for you, too: studies have shown—and guys in my workshops have attested to this—that marriages in which the father is close to the kids are less likely to end in divorce. Dads in my workshops have summed it up like this:

> My wife and I were having a lot of problems . . . If I hadn't had a strong relationship with my kids, I think we would have ended up getting divorced. I stuck with it because I knew the divorce would be awful for my kids and because I was afraid of losing time with them, even if I got joint custody. Luckily, my wife and I were able to work things out and our marriage has healed, but that may not have happened if it weren't for the kids.

> I want to spend time with the kids, but my wife gives me few opportunities to do so. It's as if she's hogging all the time with the kids, and that I can only have time with them when she feels it's appropriate.

> How can I get a chance to bond with our baby if my wife is hogging all the time with him? And how can our baby

*learn to bond with me if I hardly get a chance to spend time alone with him?*

As you can see from the first dad's comment, a strong relationship between the dad and the kids is like extra insurance for your marriage. As for the issue of trust, here's a guy you trusted enough to marry and have a child with. You should be able to trust him enough to leave the baby alone with him! A few pages from here, I'm going to share with you one of my favorite stories about leaving a dad alone with a baby, but first, let me tell you about two things that can happen while your husband is alone with the kids:

## Roughhousing and Other Bonding Activities with Dad

Bonding with Dad often includes roughhousing and healthy competition:

> *When I get home from work, my son is just waiting for me to chase after him! I'll make a quick move toward him, and he'll crack up and take off down the hall.*

> *My wife usually reads to our six-year-old son and five-year-old daughter, but I typically let them jump on me.*

Some women worry that dads roughhouse too much, or influence the kids to be too competitive. Personally, I'm a big practical joker, love to roughhouse with my kids, and have always been a sports lover—all of which I've enjoyed sharing with my boys. (It's important for dads to share these interactions with their daughters, too.) My wife Tina, like many moms, was at first worried that I would hurt the kids physically with too much roughhousing, or hurt them emotionally with too much competition or too many practical jokes.

From the moment our boys could say, "Da-da," I started playing practical jokes on them: silly things like pointing to Matt's chest and saying, "You've got a spot there." He'd look down and I'd touch his chin and say, "Gotcha!" As they got older, I'd play the "Made-you-look" joke. For example, I'd put a fork in their bowl of cereal instead of a spoon. Or I'd take the meat out of their hamburger. Or I'd honk the horn when the boys would walk past the front of the car. I thought all my practical jokes were hilarious, but Tina thought I was humiliating the kids. For years, I tried unsuccessfully to convince her that this was my way of bonding with the kids. Finally, an episode on a family vacation convinced her that there was nothing wrong with what I was doing—that it was just healthy bonding and the boys learned from it in an appropriate way.

On a family vacation when Grant was twelve, I dropped him and Tina off with my cousin Hans and his family to check into hotel rooms at the Marriott. Meanwhile, I went to park the car in the hotel's parking structure. When I entered the lobby later, everyone had already gone up to the room. I asked the desk clerk to phone Hans' room. Grant answered the phone.

"Hey, Grant," I said. "What room number are you guys in?"

"Four twenty-five," he answered. So I took the elevator up to the fourth floor and knocked on room 425. No answer. I knocked a second time. No answer. After I knocked the third time, I realized I'd been had! Grant had given me the wrong room number on purpose. Needless to say, he had a good laugh. He had grown into a teen with a healthy, creative sense of humor and knew the joke he was playing was funny, but not humiliating or dangerous. He'd learned what kinds of jokes were acceptable and had stayed within those limits. Even though he laughed his head off, there was one person who laughed even harder . . . Tina!

Other dads have told me that they have a familiar conflict with their wives when it comes to roughhousing or playing practical jokes:

> *I've tried to tell my wife that the roughhousing I do with my kids helps them understand the boundary between what is acceptable and not acceptable. They also learn self-control. If they get too rough, I'll ask them to settle down. If they continue to get too rough, I'll stop the game.*

> *My wife has a tendency to pamper our three-year-old boy too much. When he falls down, she wants to rush over and make sure he is okay. I know by his cry and how he fell that he'll be fine. So I take my time helping him because I want to give him a chance to work through falling and getting back up on his own.*

> *My wife thinks my practical jokes will hurt our daughter's self-esteem. I think they teach her how to be mentally alert and how to develop a sense of humor while learning not to take things too far.*

As these dads have explained, competition, humor, roughhousing, and practical jokes are not just pointless fun that your husband gets to have with the kids while you get stuck cooking dinner: they actually have a didactic, or educational, purpose. Kids need a chance to develop creativity and a sense of humor. Competition and sports, when taught appropriately, don't necessarily teach kids to focus on winning, but to learn to think from other people's points of view, to anticipate others' actions, and to survive in competitive situations throughout their lives, whether they win or lose. Roughhousing teaches kids the limits of physical play so that they don't hurt themselves or others.

Some moms might feel that if the kids are hurt while Dad is taking care of them, it will still be the mom's fault. This is absolutely untrue, and you should not feel guilty about things that are beyond your control. If you are having trouble with guilt, read more about it in Chapter 8.

And as you'll see in Chapter 10, dads do things a little differently than moms do, but that doesn't make fathering wrong or hurtful. Kids need both comfort and roughhousing. They need words of caution balanced out by encouragement to push themselves. They need quiet, introspective activities as well as active, physical activities. They need a mom *and* a dad.[†]

## Punishment and Discipline

This is another important issue that dads and moms don't always see eye-to-eye on. Many dads in my workshops have been frustrated about this:

> *When it comes to discipline, I do it based on rules. My wife gets all emotional because she bases it on how the punishment is going to affect her relationship with our*

---

[†]Of course, it goes without saying that in some families these roles are reversed: dad is the quiet nurturer and mom is the competitive joker, and that's just fine.

*daughter. Sometimes I feel that whenever I'm punishing my kid, I'm also punishing my wife. I say that because each time I discipline my kid, I get the cold shoulder from my wife and I'm in the doghouse for two days.*

*When I discipline, there's no compromise—a rule is a rule. You break it, and here comes the judge. And that's me . . . I'm not going to allow my wife or son to plea bargain with me for a lighter sentence.*

*I understand my wife's overprotective nature. But I don't think she understands or appreciates why I'm so hard on our kids. I'd rather she support me when I lay the law of the land on my kids, and if she doesn't agree with me, talk to me about it later, away from the kids. That way it wouldn't undermine what I do as a dad. It also gives me time to cool off. After we discuss it behind closed doors, I'd have no problem admitting it if I were wrong or too harsh. I just don't want her to make me look like a fool in front of the kids.*

*Emily dawdles before getting ready for bed. But I let her manage her own time, and if she's not in her pajamas by bedtime, I just won't read her a bedtime story. My wife, however, is more inclined to continually remind her to get moving, and then will let things slide if Emily doesn't make the deadline.*

I've seen over the years that the dads in my classes, no matter how nurturing and involved they are, tend to be stricter than moms when it comes to discipline, but that doesn't mean they want to play the bad guy, as we saw in Chapter 5. I've experienced this myself.

On a Thursday evening when he was twelve, Grant broke a rule: he and his friend Joey stayed out past their curfew and were not at the pizza parlor where they'd agreed to wait for me to pick them up. I had to spend thirty minutes looking for them and I was really worried. When I finally found them walking on the sidewalk two blocks away, I told Grant he was grounded until Saturday morning. He got upset and argued that the punishment was unfair.

"But Dad!" he protested. "There's a school dance on Friday night and I was going to go to it!"

"A rule is a rule," I said. "And you broke it."

When we got home, he appealed to Tina, who felt bad that he was going to miss the dance. She attempted to negotiate a deal with me. "Why don't we let him go to the dance and then ground him on Saturday and Sunday?" she asked.

I said no and told her that it was not negotiable. I was upset at Tina for not supporting me. I was also frustrated that she wouldn't allow me to play my role as a dad. Tina argued that my punishing Grant would harm my relationship with him. I tried to convince her that it was going to strengthen it, but Tina disagreed until the following morning.

The next morning, Grant knocked on our bedroom door. "Dad? Mom? Can I come in?"

"Sure, Grant," I said, and he opened the door. "What's up?" I asked.

Grant hung back behind the door, and I could tell he was ashamed of what he'd done, but he looked me right in the eye. "You were right, Dad. I don't deserve to go to the dance tonight."

"Thanks, Grant," I said. "It means a lot to me for you to say that."

He had obviously been thinking about what he'd done and come to the conclusion that staying out past curfew and not meeting me where he said he would was wrong. And that's exactly what I wanted him to realize by punishing him, so the punishment served its purpose.

I feel my role is to give my children a taste of what the real world is like and how harsh it can be. I uphold justice and fairness based on rules, not on my relationship with my kids, because I want to teach them that their attitudes and behaviors and the choices they make have consequences. I also enforce rules systematically and sternly to teach them right from wrong. Inconsistency would be confusing and would undermine the whole point. A proverb I shared with all of our boys is still posted in Matt's room:

> *There's a choice you have to make*
> *in everything you do.*
> *You must always keep in mind*
> *the choice you make makes you.*

I told Tina that it wasn't easy or fun for me to punish Grant. I wanted him to go to the dance and enjoy it as much as she and Grant did! I felt awful about punishing him, but I knew I was doing the right thing. No dad wants to deprive his child of having fun, but sometimes we have to because that's our job as parents.

## Back to Bonding: A Dad and His Baby Girl

Just like you need one-on-one time with your baby or child, your husband does, too. Here's the story I've been waiting to share with you. This one has stuck with me for years!

At one of my workshops for new and expectant dads, I

was mediating a dialogue about balancing childcare when a new dad arrived late, carrying his eight-week-old daughter and all of the gear: baby carrier, diaper bag, carrying pouch. I could see that the new dad, Steve, was stressed because he was sweating and didn't meet my eyes. I watched as Steve found a seat outside of the circle of expectant dads in the hospital conference room. The baby started to fuss and kick, and Steve took her from her carrier, looking panicked.

Because I try to be laid-back and welcoming in all of my classes, I called out, "Hey, Steve! Good to have you back!" I explained to the other men, "Steve came to the workshop three months ago as an expectant dad, just like you guys."

The other dads smiled and turned their curious faces toward Steve, who was now mixing formula madly as the baby began to cry, then scream. The underarms of his T-shirt were growing dark. The class went back to the discussion, but I kept one eye on Steve.

He offered the bottle, but the baby wouldn't take it. He burped her, checked her diaper, loosened her onesie, talked softly to her, rocked her. Sweat ran down his temples—it looked like he was having an anxiety attack. Nothing he tried worked, and the baby screamed so loudly that some of the expectant dads in the circle were beginning to look nervous and uncomfortable. Steve must have noticed, too, because he suddenly packed up the baby and all of her gear and ran out of the conference room, looking bummed.

"Can you guys excuse me a minute?" I asked the other dads. "I'll be right back." I went looking for Steve.

He was in an alcove in the hallway, struggling to soothe the baby and put her in her carrier. Dozens of helpful sugges-tions flew to my mind, but I had a feeling that only one thing could help Steve: letting him succeed at taking care of his daughter *on his own*.

On a hunch, I asked, "I'll bet this is the first time you've ever been alone with her, isn't it?"

He finally met my eyes. "Yeah, it is," he answered. "I don't know what to do—I've tried everything and she won't stop crying! I guess I'll just go home and let my wife take care of her, because I'm obviously no good at this."

I quickly realized that showing Steve up by fixing the situation for him was not going to help matters. Instead, I assured him that he could handle the delicate situation. "That's not true," I pointed out. "I've been watching you, and you're doing an amazing job."

Steve didn't look convinced. "She *never* screams like this when my wife holds her." He took a cell phone from the diaper bag pocket. "I'll call my wife and see if she has any suggestions."

"What's your wife doing this morning?" I asked over the baby's cries.

"She said she was going to take a shower and a nap."

"Do you think she's feeling pretty tired?" I asked.

"Oh, yeah, she's exhausted," Steve answered.

"Then how about if you stick with it and let her have a few hours alone?" I suggested. "You're doing a great job, just trust yourself. Take your time and come on back to the class whenever you're ready."

"I don't know," Steve said. He tried to give the baby the bottle again, but she turned her head and kept right on crying.

"Come on, you can do it!" I said. "The other dads and I will be pulling for you!"

Steve shook his head as if to say, *Don't get your hopes up.* I went back into the conference room, where one guy was explaining how he was really looking forward to playing with his baby, but was worried he wouldn't ever have time to bond with his kid between work and other obligations.

Ten minutes later, one of the conference room doors eased open. Steve stepped through quietly, holding the baby carrier in one hand. The carrier was draped with a soft pink blanket, and I grinned and gave him the thumbs-up sign and Steve sat down and joined the discussion while the baby slept.

I knew that Steve had gained the confidence he needed to be a great dad, and I knew that Steve, his wife, and his daughter would all benefit from that confidence for a lifetime. But I wondered if Steve's wife knew how difficult the day had been for her husband, or how much he had grown. Steve is a perfect example of a dad needing to be alone with his kid, and he was a huge motivation for me to write this book!

### Hogan's Slogan #17: "It's the 'what,' not the 'how.'"

The number-one reason men feel their wives don't appreciate their parenting skills? These dads say moms focus too much on *how* they accomplish tasks, not *what* they accomplish. As you can see from Steve's powerful story, sometimes *what* is enough by itself!

Such issues continue well into childhood and throughout years of even the most successful marriages. In fact, it was a big issue in my own house, and I'm a stay-at-home dad. How our kids were dressed is a prime example of the what/how issue.

When my kids were little and I dressed them in the mornings, I used two criteria for choosing their clothes:

a.  Is it hot outside?
b.  Is it cold outside?

To me, the important thing was that the kids were dressed and not too hot or too cold. I wasn't thinking about whether their shoes matched their socks or whether they wore the same outfit to playgroup last week. For Tina, on the other hand, how our children were dressed was an important part of measuring her worth as a good mother. It was a perspective I couldn't relate to at first, but I learned to understand how important it was for her.

Because Tina worked, I would get the kids up in the mornings, dole out cereal or make pancakes, and get them dressed. I thought that this would be a relief to her and a way of making things easy on her in the mornings so she could get dressed and get herself out the door. Later on, it was a huge help to her, but at first we had arguments that went like this:

"He's not wearing *that* to preschool, is he?" Tina asked, pointing at four-year-old Grant, who was eating pancakes with Wesley and wearing an outfit Tina felt didn't match.

"Uh . . . it looks like he's wearing it to me," I answered.

"Honey, that clashes. And he's wearing the T-shirt he slept in."

I looked at Grant's clothes. He looked like a happy four-year-old who was wearing one of his favorite outfits. "Nobody's going to know he slept in that shirt. Besides, this is the outfit he chose to wear to school."

"What are people going to think about parents who let their kid go out the door like that?" she asked.

"That we're cool because we let him choose his own clothes every once in awhile?" I asked. "It's not like he's going to church or a formal party."

She put her coffee cup down. "I guess I'll have to dress him," she said. "Come on, Grant."

I surrendered because I didn't want Tina and Grant to be late.

"Aw, Mom!" Grant said, but he followed her. I could hear them talking and dresser drawers opening and closing in Grant's room. I served myself some pancakes and sat down with Wesley, our other son, who was too little to do much but watch. I didn't *feel* cool. I felt like an idiot, and I was confused and hurt.

Finally, they came back out with Grant wearing a new outfit.

"Please make sure he also takes a sweatshirt to school. It's a little chilly outside," Tina said.

While Tina was satisfied with the way the morning went, Grant and I weren't. Grant was unhappy because he didn't get to wear the clothes he chose. I was unhappy and frustrated for a couple of reasons. First, although Tina had agreed to relinquish the childcare duties to me, it seemed she wasn't comfortable doing so, and that she didn't appreciate my efforts and couldn't accept the way I cared for the boys.

Second, I was confused because I thought the whole idea of my involvement was to give Tina peace of mind and lighten her workload. Instead, it caused more conflict.

I was in a quandary as to why she wasn't enjoying her newfound freedom from some of her motherly duties, and I wondered if she appreciated the quality time we were spending as a family. Here I was making every effort to be an involved and responsible father, and she was taking that responsibility away from me.

Later, we talked about the situation and Tina realized she needed to trust me with the parenting duties. Over time, we've worked out problems like this and they aren't as much of an issue now. But it took years of practice for me to explain my feelings and for Tina to let go of *how* our kids were dressed and be satisfied, and even pleased, to see that they *were* dressed each morning . . . and were not too hot or too cold, but just right.

Dads in my classes have confided to me that they also feel frustrated and stressed about living up to their wives' expectations of *how* things should be done at home. Making a dad feel inept as a caregiver doesn't help motivate him to be a caregiver. Being critical of how a dad diapers, dresses a child, or cooks discourages him from doing these things. Dads are capable of taking care of babies and kids, just as moms are capable of working outside of the home. Both need a little support and encouragement from their spouses to feel successful and motivated. Dads say:

> *I wish my wife would trust and confide in me, relatives, friends, and neighbors more often to help care for the children.*

> *I'd like to see my wife not let the way she is dressed or our child is dressed or what kind of clothes they are wearing define her role as a mother. It's okay for our kids to not be color-coordinated.*

I've chosen to use color coordination as an example here because it seems to be really important to many moms, including my wife. Once I realized this, I made an effort to learn how to color coordinate so that on important occasions, the kids would be dressed nicely, but Tina also compromised by looking the other way most days. She came to realize that it's the *what*, not the *how*—that it's more important that the kids be dressed, fed, and happy than whether or not their clothes match or they used spoons for their pancakes instead of forks.

Ultimately, allowing your husband to participate in the parenting duties will give him more confidence in his role as a dad, will help with the kids' development, will strengthen the relationships of everyone in the family. Also, it will result in less stress for you, which I'll talk about further in Chapter 8.

## Dad's Play-by-Play: What to Know from Chapter 6

- Remember that your husband may have fewer hours per week to learn parenting skills.

- Don't give to-do lists when leaving your husband alone with the kids. Let him figure it out.

- If you're expecting a baby, start involving your husband in childcare duties now.

- Allow your husband one-on-one time with the kids.

- Remember that "dad" play, such as roughhousing and practical jokes, is important to your child's development.

- Uphold your husband's discipline measures for your children's sake and for your husband's sake. If you disagree, discuss it later, away from the kids.

- Trust your husband with the baby or kids—he's their dad!

- Focus on *what* your husband is doing, not *how* he's doing it.

- Let color coordination and dressing errors slide.

- Smile and encourage him when he spends time with the kids.

# WE CAN TAKE CARE
# OF THE HOUSEHOLD!

During a workshop I asked a group of moms the following question: "Please answer honestly. How many of you—without hesitation—could take a weekend getaway right now and leave your husband to take care of the house with no instructions, and when you return accept whatever condition the house and kids are in?" None of the moms raised their hands.

By the end of this chapter, you will be able to answer "Yes" to that question.

I'm a lucky man. Tina has allowed me to be at home with the kids for fifteen years, and the house has never burned down. The kids are still breathing. But this degree of comfort came from a combination of our efforts and compromises, as well as chance circumstances that shaped our life and our views.

Many moms experience lifelong frustration about their husband's disengagement from household chores. There are many theories about why men can't, won't, or just don't pitch in, but there are a lot of men who *do*, and those men can help shed some valuable light on the marital conflicts surrounding housework. The purpose of this chapter is to let you in on how men really feel about housework and their image, how they feel about their wives' concept of housework, and finally, share some recommendations on how to get your husband more involved in housework in the section titled "Can he? Yes. But *will* he?"

## How Men Really Feel about Housework and the Male Image

I have met a lot of men over the years who do more than half of the housework. I'm one of them. But for each of us dads who washes dishes, mops floors, folds laundry, and scrubs toilets on a regular basis, there have been some tough self-evaluation gymnastics to go through first. By sharing these insights with you, I hope to spare you and your husband some of the double-back handsprings.

The first somersault we turned was over the Bumbling Dad media image Hollywood has portrayed over the last twenty years. Probably the most famous Bumbling Dad was brought to viewers in the 1983 movie *Mr. Mom*, starring Michael Keaton. Keaton's character is completely clueless about childcare, but he doesn't need to worry for long, because his wife eventually quits her job and takes over again. In the meantime, though, there are lots of hijinks that feature him stapling a security blanket together and making a mess with dinner.

While I understood the humor and intentions of Hollywood to produce a movie about role reversal between a working father and stay-at-home mother, *Mr. Mom* subsequently did more harm than good by painting an image of incompetence in the new role men were asked to play as househusbands in the 1990s. Further complicating this issue is the fact that our culture promotes the notion that cleaning house is women's work and that a man's place is in the garage.

My transition from running a wallpaper installation business and operating a heavy-duty Shop Vac that sucks up nails and chunks of wood to a lightweight Hoover vacuum cleaner was not easy. It was like asking me to trade in a Porsche for a Plymouth. In addition to having to operate an unfamiliar piece of equipment, I also had to perform a task that was emotionally foreign to me. The thought of going from wearing a tool belt to an apron also did not appeal to me. In the beginning, I admit that I did look like a bumbling buffoon—even without the apron. However, it didn't take long for me to master the art of vacuuming. This was also true of all the other household tasks: I got off to a rough start, but over time, I could do them very well.

Other stay-at-home dads I know have had the same experience. At first, taking care of the household is more work because they're still learning how to do it, and many of them aren't comfortable enough in their new role to admit they are the primary caregiver . . . the running joke is that they haven't "come out of the pantry."

The main reason most men are embarrassed to admit their at-home dad status or that they partake in household chores has little to do with their comfort level and a lot to do with having to put up with being the butt of jokes. The involved dads I know take their role as househusbands very seriously and do it with great pride. For them, this is no joking matter.

Here are some comments from other fathers who are offended by the bumbling dad image:

*As a young father, I hate the stereotype you often see on television and commercials of the bumbling dad. Does it take us a touch longer to pick up some skills when it comes to child-rearing? Sure, but that doesn't mean that we remain bumbling for the rest of our lives.*

*I know I'm not the only guy out there who is getting a little tired of the bumbling dad image. I know quite a few men, like me, who are quite capable of maintaining a clean and orderly household. Just ask my wife. Or better yet, drop by our home for a visit.*

*It seems that the point of most sitcoms that portray bumbling dads is that if mom doesn't get better soon the children will starve and the house will fall apart.*

*I get a little fed up with the bumbling dad image I constantly see on TV. I wonder what would happen if the situation were reversed? I'm sure it wouldn't take long for letters of complaints to pile up for denigrating motherhood on TV.*

*I'm the stay-at-home parent and I get labeled as Mr. Mom. Funny thing is, I've never heard anyone call my wife, the breadwinner, Mrs. Dad. Hey, that's a good title for a sitcom.*

*It is unfair to women to "mom"ify the job. Calling a guy "Mr. Mom" implies mom should be the one behind the stroller. That ought to be pretty offensive nowadays.*

*Hollywood and the advertising industry have, for years now, had what seems to be a policy of portraying men as either bad guys, losers, idiots, or at least the butt of the jokes.*

*Don't call me Mr. Mom. Our boys already have a mother. I'm not a replacement for mom. I'm a dad.*

*Is anybody else getting tired of doofus dad comedies? I don't know about you, but I'm pretty sure I've seen every emasculating joke there could be about stereotypically incompetent men being left alone with their kids and bungling everything while their wives are away.*

*Being a SAHD [stay-at-home dad], I find that many people are more open to giving me some leniency. Which can be a bit of a double-edged sword. It's good for me—hey, let's forgive the well-meaning but somewhat bumbling dad.*

*Sitcom dads in the past twenty years have progressively gotten dumber, while mothers have become the smart ones in the virtual family. We spend twice as much time with our kids as we did two decades ago, but on television dads are oblivious, troubled, deranged, and generally incompetent. Even if dad has a good job, like the star of* Home Improvement, *at home he's forever making messes that must be straightened out by mom.*

I've also met many wives who hate the stereotype of the Bumbling Dad. These moms have no problem admitting that their husbands are as capable or more capable than they are at managing the household. Many of these moms are working wives of at-home dads.

As the dads noted, the stereotype is a staple of many TV shows and sitcoms. The classic *Mr. Mom* sums up this topic in a nutshell.

A more recent example of a bumbling dad in film is the remake of *Cheaper by the Dozen* starring Steve Martin. Though it was based on a much older book, the movie differs greatly from the original Depression-era story. A monkey wrench is thrown in the Baker family's routine when the wife and mother of twelve—count 'em, twelve—kids goes off on a book tour and leaves the working dad in charge. Somehow, Kate, the mom, has managed to smoothly run a household of twelve kids on her own while writing a book, but Tom, her husband, can't make dinner or keep the kids in line while she's gone.

TV's Homer Simpson, one of the most popular and beloved sitcom dads, has shown his extreme ineptness by losing the baby, Maggie, in more than one episode! A common dynamic in the family consists of Homer making a mess out of a situation and Marge bailing him out. Or what about Ray of *Everybody Loves Raymond*? He's another funny dad without a clue. Even though Ray works out of the home, he's rarely shown taking care of the kids or the household, tasks which are left to his wife, Debra, or his own mom. In one episode, Debra suggests that Ray spend more time with the kids, so he takes them to basketball practice. Ray winds up in a fight with the coach . . . of course, Debra is there to save the day.

In *Malcolm in the Middle*, Hal and Lois have four boys, the oldest of whom is in his late teens. You'd think with so many years of parenthood under his belt that Hal could handle an afternoon alone with his kids, but no, when Hal is supposed to watch Joe's cat, he pays his youngest son, Dewey, to do it instead. Of course, chaos ensues when Dewey loses the cat and lets in dozens of other animals through an open window. So how is the episode resolved? Lois finds out and fixes everything.

These stereotypes are damaging to dads, and ultimately, to moms and kids as well. They offend dads and teach women that they are required to stay at the helm of household duties or the house will literally come crashing down. They teach kids that their fathers are idiots and their mothers have endless patience for idiocy.

The second somersault we have to turn is over our masculinity. Traditionally, housework has been viewed as the woman's domain, so a guy might have doubts about his manhood when he picks up a basket of laundry for the first time. Maybe the doubts are small, or maybe they're expressed more aggressively, like, "Hey, why am *I* stuck with laundry? This isn't my job! I'm a man!" Unfortunately, men's egos are very fragile when it comes to this subject, so he probably won't come right out and say, "Honey, sorting laundry makes me feel like less of a man."

Some women and men have told me that men really are Bumbling Dads when it comes to housework. I think there are two reasons men can act this way. First, if Bumbling Dads are held up by our society as manly, then men might not feel comfortable being competent in household chores because they feel it jeopardizes their manhood. For example, if a guy believes that "real" men are rough and messy in the house, then he might make a huge, messy Dagwood sandwich, and, while he's at it, use the biggest knife in the drawer to slice the tomatoes. His wife is left cleaning up the mess and scratching her head. But when it comes to tying fishing lines or other "manly" activities, the husband shows he can be dextrous and detail-oriented.

Likewise, a woman I know played possum when it came to changing the headlight in her car. She told me, "It's dirty. It's greasy. I don't think it's my job to change the headlights. It's his job!" But this same woman did a number on her garden that spring, using big tools, pushing heavy wheelbarrows, and wearing holes in the knees of her jeans. The catch is that gardening was a more comfortable activity for her because it was a "womanly" activity.

Combining the fact that men unconsciously view housework as women's work with the illusion that men are incompetent makes for a very difficult situation, but one that husbands and wives can work through.

At the end of my first book, I juxtaposed a list from Bruce Feirstein's *Real Men Don't Eat Quiche* with a list of my own, "the List of a Real Dad." Feirstein's book reaffirmed all of the macho stereotypes, starting with "Real men don't eat quiche . . . they eat meat and potatoes," and so on, ad infinitum. I said in my own list that a real dad thinks it's not only okay to eat quiche, but to cook it as well. Today, I'm taking that statement one step further:

> Hogan's Slogan #40: "Real men are not afraid of quiche or stereotypes."

I'm comfortable with my manhood. A little quiche or a macho stereotype is not going to scare me into conforming to somebody else's stereotypes.

The second reason that a dad might actually bumble around the house is that he might be learning some household skills for the first time. It takes time and trust to get him into the swing of things.

"No," some moms say, "my husband doesn't let any of those stereotypes faze him. He just flat-out doesn't care about the state of the house." Maybe he doesn't care; perhaps he used to. And what if, just what if, his view on the household is a healthy one that you would enjoy?

## Dads' Take on Their Wives' Concept of Housework

As many moms have pointed out to me, dads' approach to housework is quite different than their wives,' and therein lies the crux of conflict. It's largely in the *what*, not the *how*, as with issues of childcare (see Chapter 6). Time and again, I've heard frustration from dads and moms who don't see eye to eye on housework and who have reached a point where they can't even talk about it without the dialogue degenerating into a heated argument, let alone work out a reasonable compromise.

When it comes to pitching in around the house, many men feel like they're damned if they do and damned if they don't because they have to live up to their wives' standards of housekeeping. A dad once told me, "We men hold back our feelings because we don't want to deal with the drama we get from our wives and girlfriends."

I'm reminded of a strip from the *For Better or For Worse* comic by Lynn Johnston in which Elly, the mother, follows her husband around while he's cleaning house and corrects him on the details. "Oh, John," she says, "When you load the dishwasher, the plates go *this* way 'round." She leans over and flips the plates around herself, oblivious to her husband's expression of irritation. The last panel shows her talking to her friend over coffee and saying that John is a wonderful husband, but she can't figure out why he doesn't help out more around the house. The cartoonist, a woman who has said her strip closely mirrors her real-life family, was throwing light on the importance of focusing on the *what*.

Dads agree with this. For us, the point of doing housework is for it to get done.

Take Tina and me as an example. Tina has laundry down to a fine art: she divides it by very dirty and semi-dirty, and washes towels, delicates, and black separately. Personally, I just make sure not to wash the whites with the reds. Over the years, Tina's come to a place where she's happy that I'm doing the laundry and that she doesn't have to do as much of it. But that didn't happen overnight—we argued a lot first. Other dads share their conflicts:

*Sarah gave me a list of five things to do around the house while she was gone for the day. I only got two of them done because I was too busy having fun with the girls. When she came home I was in the middle of braiding Katie's hair. Instead of appreciating the time she had to herself and our father/daughter moment, Sarah went off on me in front of the kids for not meeting her expectations of a clean house . . . She also made me look bad in front of the kids.*

*My wife gets frustrated with me because the house isn't as clean as she would like it to be. She reminds me how clean and organized she keeps the house. I hate it when she does that. I admit that she is better at managing the household. But that's because she spends more time at home alone while I'm at work. I think she forgets to take that into consideration.*

*Kelly says that I don't do enough housework and if I do more, that I'll get more sex. I tell her that I think I do a fair share and that if she gives me more sex, I'll do more housework. I feel like we're in a Mexican stand-off.*

*When Diane leaves me alone with the kids on the weekend, she's always busting my chops and manages to find something I did wrong or didn't do. Somehow she's forgotten that I hired a maid service—with my hard-earned money—to help her around the house during the weekdays.*

*Learning how to manage the household has been similar to learning how to care for a newborn baby. It took a while to get the hang of it. It's been quite a juggling act coordinating the laundry, mopping, vacuuming, cooking, especially with two crumb-crunchers in tow . . . I think I've managed to do a pretty good job. But if you talk with my wife, she'd tell you otherwise.*

*If anyone knows how hard it is to juggle two kids and keep the house in order, it's my wife. So why can't she cut me a little slack?*

To sum up these comments: dads have less time than moms to learn to juggle household chores and childcare, they place priority on playing with their kids if that time is limited, and they feel that if anyone should understand how difficult this balance is, it's their wives.

Another dad told me once, "You know what, Hogan?

I think that my wife sees the house as an extension of herself. If the house isn't in perfect order, she thinks it's a reflection of her as a person." For a mom, relinquishing a part of the household duties can be just as difficult as it was to relinquish the care of the baby. Often, this situation can turn into a major control issue that colors discussions of which dishes can go into the dishwasher and which ones can't, and dads throw up their hands in exasperation.

I've listened to hundreds of dads and moms spew their frustration on this topic, and I've given it a lot of thought. I think that the heart of the issue may lie even deeper in the marital ribcage.

Let me venture another possible reason women want their husbands to live up to high standards: to better appreciate what they as women go through each day. That is, maybe some moms want the housework done, but maybe that's not all they want—maybe some moms keep their standards high so their husbands will understand just how much drudgery housework can be and finally appreciate them more.

Have you done this? If so, maybe it's time to turn your own somersault. Reflect on your reasons for asking your husband to pitch in more. Ask yourself honestly, "Would I be happy if he did housework his way? Or am I setting unattainable standards? If so, is my reason for setting those standards so that he will appreciate me more?" If the real reason is so that your husband will appreciate your work more, then there are less stressful—and more effective—ways to go about it.

---

## ♀AND A MOM WANTS YOU TO KNOW
# Saying Goodbye to the Inspectors

The expectations we have of housekeeping, whether they stem from tradition, oppression, or both, are often unattainable for us and for our husbands, and they stress everybody out. What kind of household showcase are we trying to create, anyway? It's as if the state of the house will be judged and graded by a team of inspectors wearing white jumpsuits, gloves, and goggles.

Carrying their clipboards, they enter your house through the front door, surveying the décor for coordination. "Nice watercolor above the mantel," says Inspector Smith, making a checkmark on his housework inspection form. "B+ for taste." But things go downhill from there.

"Dust on the frame!" says Inspector Jones. She runs her green-gloved finger along the edge and peers at the resulting film of dust on her glove. "It's been *months* since this place was dusted," she sneers, wiping her hand on her jumpsuit with disdain. She gives your house a D— in the dusting category.

The track on the sliding glass door could stand a washing. In the kitchen, the crack between the stove and the counter is a web of dried spaghetti sauce and melted cheese. There are dry beans scattered on the floor in the back corner of the pantry. The inspectors cluck their tongues and note these details on their forms. Upstairs, another inspector uses a patent-pending clean-o-meter to deduce that the sheets haven't been changed in two weeks. "The socks in this drawer are so disorganized," says Inspector Smith with a prim smile of satisfaction. He relishes such discoveries. "F!"

"Don't even ask about the toilet in the kids' bathroom," Jones mumbles under her breath.

At the end of the inspection, a large banner is hung from your house for all the neighborhood to see: "Household order and cleanliness: D+."

. . . or not. There are no inspectors. There's no such thing as a clean-o-meter, either. So where do these standards come from? Guys who are pitching in around the house feel like their efforts are never good enough for us. And maybe they're not, if we're expecting the house to look like it was cleaned with a Q-tip and a bottle of bleach. C'mon, no one's house is like that. Free yourself! Give the floor a good ol' bachelor mopping and call it a day. (Hogan, if you prefer, we can redefine it as "busy parent mopping.") There are better things to do in life than clean the grout with a toothbrush.

The flip side of this liberty is that we cannot judge other women by the state of their houses. Now, I have nothing against gossip in general, but if you want to be free from the unattainable standards of perfection, you can't hold other women (or men, for that matter) to them, either. Don't perpetuate the standards by gossiping about another woman's sticky floor or the cobwebs in her eaves. Don't whisper to other people, "Don't eat at her house. Last time I was there, she washed the dishes in lukewarm water."

The house—messy, clean, or in-between—belongs to both the woman and the man. What's more, unless there are mice in the hallway and mold in the sink, they probably have things under control.

## Can He? Yes. But Will He? A Three-Pronged Approach

Being a stay-at-home parent is a really, really hard job. Sometimes, in an effort to highlight her hard work and get thanks for it, a mom might emphasize how difficult and time-consuming a task like doing the laundry is by noting every single detail as she teaches her husband how to do it. I think this won't get you very far, because your husband will be overwhelmed by how complicated everything sounds. As with childcare, there's no need to tell your husband how hard it is, because he'll soon find out for himself.

The best way to get a break from the laundry, and have your husband understand how hard housework is, is to facilitate him participating in it. Make it simple: say, "Put the clothes in here. Here's how you turn the machine on. Fill it with this much soap," and then stop with the instructions.

Your husband is just as capable of household chores as he is of caring for the kids, but keep in mind that he will probably do them his way and only turn to you for help on sticking points. Sometimes, dads are open to their wives' suggestions, instructions, and advice, but only if it doesn't sound like nagging. Rather than criticize my efforts, Tina has been very encouraging, and I think that's part of why I feel confident and comfortable doing housework. I guess you can say it's paid off for her!

If, despite your efforts, it seems your husband has dug his heels into the linoleum and won't stoop to mop it, it means that your tactics, right or wrong, are not working. So you have nothing to lose by a new approach. Try my three-pronged approach: *praise, practicality,* and *patience.*

*Praise* his efforts, even if it feels like you're cheering on a high schooler for adding one plus one and coming up with two. Also praise his accomplishments and be specific. Everyone likes to be noticed for the good work they do.

Keep *practicality* in mind. Don't set high standards for him and don't give overly complicated instructions. The shorter the instructions, the better.

Be *patient.* He may take a while to learn to balance chores. As with caring for a baby, men have not been trained or given many opportunities to engage in housework before they begin their trek into marriage and fatherhood. The first day I tried to keep two loads of laundry going, cook dinner for three, and keep the baby from chewing on the TV cable, I thought I was going to pass out. I found it much harder and more tiring than playing a full-court press in basketball. Yes, dinner was late, but after a few months, I could do it with one hand tied behind my back, and I had developed a new appreciation for stay-at-home moms (and dads).

Using the three-pronged approach, you can follow these other handy tips:

- Start him off slow. If he likes to golf on the weekends, ask him to cut back from eighteen holes to nine so that he can come home and be a part of the family.
- If you don't like getting stuck with all of the household chores, don't divide all household tasks down the old male-female lines. If you don't already do so, change tires, check car fluids, and fix odd things around the house. (You can ask your husband to teach you if you want.) Then he'll be free to pitch in on other household tasks.
- If you suspect your husband resists housework because it's not "manly," try talking about it like it is. Borrow lingo from sports or business to say things like, "Can you help me **tackle** the laundry?" or "We need a **game plan** for how we're going to get dinner ready every night," or "Let's **head off** this termite situation before it gets **out of line.**" This language can help him feel more confident and comfortable with his role in the household chores.
- Turn chores into *projects*. "Project" is a more manly word than "chore."

- Reaffirm his manhood in other ways so that he's not a slave to macho stereotypes. This doesn't necessarily mean in bed, although he probably wouldn't mind. You can call him "tough," "smart," "strong," or "brave" in reference to his role as a dad and involved parent.
- Encourage his first attempts at tasks like laundry by thanking him instead of pointing out mistakes. Say, "Thanks for folding the clothes," rather than "Fold the pants in thirds instead of halves!"
- Trust him not to burn the house down. Now go on that weekend getaway and leave no instructions.

Being a team parent is good for the goose and good for the gander, and it's also good for the goslings . . . the state of the pen comes in dead last. That's what dads think in an eggshell.

## Dad's Play-by-Play: What to Know from Chapter 7

- Dads are capable of housework. Some of us are pretty darned good at it, too.
- "Bumbling Dads" are a common degrading stereotype in TV and movies.
- Dads may act like Bumbling Dads around the house to protect their manhood. You can help reduce this fear by talking about him and the chores in a way that highlights his "man appeal."
- Teasing a dad about his efforts to be involved with household chores will not help get him involved.
- Dads may appear to bumble if they're trying skills out for the first time. They'll get better with time.

- Dads throw up their hands altogether at the housework when they find they can't measure up to impossible standards.

- A dad who pitches in with the housework may not do it your way.

- Remember that the state of the household is not a reflection of you as a person.

- Your husband will not appreciate your housework more if you force him to live up to your standards; he'll just give up altogether.

- Say goodbye to imaginary inspectors who might peer down their noses at your less-than-perfect house.

- Use the three-pronged approach of *praise, practicality,* and most of all, *patience* to get your husband more involved in the housework.

# 8

# WE DON'T WANT YOU
# TO BE "SUPERMOM"

Have you ever heard of Supermom? I have. Moms in my workshops have told me all about her. Here's what I've learned about Supermom: she has an immaculate, professionally decorated house; she has smart, beautiful children; she buys every material possession she or her family could ever want; she's married to a man who is smart, handsome, fit, and makes six figures, and they get along famously; she has a lucrative side job of her own; she volunteers to help out at the kids' school twice a week; and she still manages to look great in a swimsuit after three kids!

I want all of the moms in the world to know that this creature *does not exist*. There is no such thing as a Supermom. If you think a person you know is a real-life Supermom, she probably has high blood pressure, tons of guilt, loads of credit card debt, a surgically enhanced body, never gets enough sleep, and often feels guilty, frustrated, and lonely. In other words, Supermom is an illusion.

**Hogan's Slogan #47: "Supermom does not exist."**

I once told a group of moms that Supermom does not exist, and one mom directed me to proof that Supermoms *do* exist: celebrity magazines. While standing in the checkout line at the supermarket, I've noticed that the tabloids set up near the cash registers have really focused on celebrity moms over the last few years. They show pictures of pregnant movie stars going for jogs with their bodyguards. They run articles on how a new mom with millions of dollars made the "tough" decision to stay at home for a few years with her small child. They feature photo spreads of brand-new, well-stocked nurseries, complete with flouncy bassinets, set up for a celeb's unborn baby. After the baby is born, they run a photograph of the new mom on the cover of the magazine, holding her baby and looking like, well, a movie star.

There are no doubt many celebrities who really *do* get involved with their kids and make tough decisions about giving up their exciting careers to spend more time with their kids. But that doesn't mean they're perfect. Besides, comparing yourself to these incredibly wealthy women who are portrayed as perfect in a magazine and who you don't know personally (and whose faults you therefore can't see) won't make you feel very good about yourself as a mom.

In fact, in some cases, celebrity moms are just playing the part in front of the cameras and letting their hired help do all of the hard parenting work. Nannies may be the real caretakers in the kids' lives, and professional decorators might be the ones masterminding the design of the perfect nursery. Manufacturers might give away baby gear for free if celebrities use it in public or promote it on TV. Celebrities might be portrayed as "working" moms but are only working three months a year and taking their kids with them on the road when they do work.

Some dads understand the Supermom myth. Others are totally clueless as to why their wife is frustrated and over-worked, even after Dad has taken on extra duties so that Mom can have more free time. But all of the guys are shocked at how far their wives will go to attain this ideal. In 2003, I asked dads in my workshops to name one thing they would like their wives to do, and almost all of them wanted their wives to stop playing Supermom. I got more responses than I expected! Here are just a few of the many, many comments guys made on this subject:

*I'd like to see my wife stop feeling guilty about making time for herself.*

*I'd like to see my wife take naps when our baby takes a nap and forget about cleaning the house.*

*I wish my wife would let our kids be kids and not put so much pressure on their academic performance.*

*I wish my wife would let our kids, as they grow older, do their own homework, school projects, and more around the house.*

*I'd like to see my wife get the kids involved in age-appropriate household tasks.*

*I wish my wife wouldn't get so wrapped up in her to-do list and feel a sense of accomplishment at the end of the day, even if she was only able to get to five of the ten things she had on her list.*

*I wish my wife wouldn't over-schedule and make sure that there is plenty of time to get where she needs to be.*

*I'd like to see my wife cut down on the amount of activities she plans for our children.*

*I wish she wouldn't worry so much about our child's grades in school.*

*I'd like to see my wife choose simplicity over multiplicity. Keep it simple and don't try to do what it would take five people to do. Giving the best of you is the most important thing that you can offer.*

*I don't like to see my wife try to do more than she is capable of doing.*

*I wish my wife wouldn't always feel like she has to put makeup on.*

*I'd like to see my wife recognize she is one person. If she wears herself down, she won't have the strength or energy to help anyone.*

*I'd like to see my wife not try to be all things to all people.*

*I'd like to see my wife cut down on the multitasking.*

*I'd like to see my wife not try to be the perfect mom, but to just be around.*

*I'd like to see my wife stop operating in overdrive.*

*I wish my wife would focus on all the good things she does for the family.*

*I think my wife should pat herself on the back more often.*

*I wish my wife would have fun being a mom!*

Like I said, these are just a few of the comments I got. I know lots of moms who push themselves too hard. For example, one day at our boys' elementary school, I walked into the multipurpose room to check out some of the model missions that were turned in. It was obvious that most of the elaborate projects were built from kits and put together by adults. No elementary school child can make a perfect miniature replica of the San Juan Bautista mission to scale, complete with realistic, two-inch-tall people made by hand from papier mâché. Moms who do their kids' schoolwork are like dads who try to live vicariously through their kids in sports. In both cases, the parent is acting on their own need for self-validation, and the kid winds up feeling pressured and misses out on the fun and learning experience of the activity.

Judging from the amount of responses to my questionnaire, this is a really important issue to dads who love their wives and would like them to be less stressed out and not try to live up to the Supermom myth. Let's talk about some ways to replace the myth with facts.

## Replacing the Myth with Facts

Remember that Supermom is a mythical creature. Don't let guilt or outside pressures force you into a situation in which you're overworked and frustrated. If you're finding yourself stressed out because the bathroom fixtures aren't gleaming, your husband's take on it might very well be, "Who cares? Let the bathroom get a little more dirty. We can clean it next week."[†]

Frustration and guilt set in when you can't turn ideals into reality. Here are some ideals that moms have identified for me, and the reality of each situation for most moms.

| Ideal | Reality |
| --- | --- |
| An immaculate and well-decorated house | Kids live in your house |
| Well-behaved, smart, over-achieving children | Kids are only human, and they don't respond well to pressure |
| Every material possession you or your family could want | Credit card debt |
| A husband who looks like a movie star and makes as much money | Dads, like moms and kids, are only human (See Chapter 9 for more on Superdads) |
| A perfect marriage | A healthy relationship *isn't* perfect—it has conflict sometimes |
| A lucrative side job | Networking and building up a business takes a lot of time |
| Volunteering twice a week at the kids' school | It's okay to say no |
| A body like Carmen Electra | Carmen Electra has never given birth |

---

[†]And if his take on the bathroom is, "This bathroom is filthy—stop slacking and get to work!" try saying, "I'm too tired and stressed out to clean it right now. If you want me to clean it now, I won't be able to make dinner. Otherwise, I'll clean it next week."

Dads hate to see their wives kill themselves in an attempt to attain these ideals. Perfection doesn't exist. I repeat: *perfection does not exist.*

You may find that your husband—and maybe your kids—not only worry about your attempts to be a Supermom, but that they don't even appreciate the extra effort it takes. It might be that the extra mile you're going is better spent on yourself if you're the only one who appreciates it. If the extra mile is in vain, as with some of the birthday parties I've heard about at Proud Dads workshops, you should ask yourself *why* you're trying to be a Supermom. If your husband and kids don't appreciate your efforts, and you're stressed and overworked to boot, who does it benefit? Nobody. Don't feel guilty for not being perfect.

I've heard about some pretty elaborate birthday parties over the years, but Robert's story stands out in particular. While we were discussing the Supermom myth in one of the workshops, Robert told the group that his wife, Meredith, went overboard with their son Todd's sixth birthday.

Robert told us that Meredith took time to make it a memorable event: there was a cartoon theme, a huge, air-brushed cake, and tons of presents. There was a bubble-blowing machine, a karaoke machine, and an inflatable jump house. There were goodie bags that had to be made for the guests ahead of time. "What seemed like little expenses all added up—the party cost over five hundred dollars—"

"Five hundred bucks!" yelped one of the other dads. "Ouch!"

"—and the planning took up Meredith's free time for a month."

"Whatever happened to a simple birthday party?" asked another dad in the class.

"I have no idea," Robert answered. "But wait, there's more: I hadn't even realized that there had to be another birthday party for Todd at school. Meredith wanted to bake cupcakes, but she didn't have time, so she had to buy them. She thought storebought cupcakes were lesser cupcakes and that it was some kind of failure on her part that she didn't make them at home. Then, she had to buy decorations, plates, and utensils for thirty kids and rush to the school to drop all of it off in the morning."

"Did Todd like the parties?" I asked.

Robert shrugged. "He seemed happy, but not ecstatic. He was like, 'Thanks, Mom.' Seriously, I have no idea why she killed herself over the birthday. It was expensive and time-consuming, and if Todd didn't care that much, why did she?"

Other dads added their concerns to the discussion. They felt like all the wives' effort were wasted if the kids didn't appreciate the results. They wanted to see their wives spend their free time recharging their batteries and taking care of themselves, not bending over backwards for birthday parties. They also said that expensive birthday parties put more pressure on them to work harder and bring home more money, as we saw in Chapter 3.

After the workshop ended, I didn't think much about Robert, Meredith, or the birthday party until one day a year and half later while I was grocery shopping. As I stood poking at styrofoam trays of steaks, somebody said, "Hey, Hogan!" and I turned around.

It was Robert. "Hey," he said, "thanks for mediating that

discussion on Supermoms last year. It really helped me think about the pressure on my wife to be a Supermom."

"Sure, no problem!" I said. "How are things now?"

"Well," he answered, "I've tried to take some of that pressure off of her, and I think she and Todd appreciate it. For Todd's seventh birthday, I asked Meredith if I could organize and coordinate his party. She said yes, but couldn't really keep from intervening and helping out. She started giving me advice on what to do because she wanted everything to be perfect. I told her it would be perfect however it turned out, and that it would be the way Todd wanted it to be. I still gave in to letting her buy the cake and make the goodie bags.

"Then I asked Todd what *he* wanted to do for his birthday. He said he just wanted to have fun, and asked me to build an obstacle course in the backyard. He didn't want any frills, and I decided that this was going to be a low-budget party." To serve the cake, Robert told me that he used a hodgepodge of paper plates and napkins that they already had in the house. It was a mix of different themes and characters, and even some plain white plates and clear plastic utensils. He set up the obstacle course using only items he had around the house, like extra tires and empty boxes. He didn't impose a schedule on the birthday party, either: the kids ran through the obstacle course, laughing like crazy. When they got hungry, he served the cake. When they got tired, they sat down.

"Guess which birthday party was the most fun and memorable for Todd?" he asked me.

"The one without the frills," I answered.

"You got it."

Robert inspected a roast, then threw it in his basket. "The stress and expense of trying to be a Supermom just doesn't pay off. Those elaborate birthday parties aren't worth it."

I nodded, and we said goodbye. I went back to my shopping, thinking over what Robert had told me and how I might incorporate it into the next workshop. Just as I was about to head to the produce section, Robert approached me again. "Hey, Hogan, there's something else I want to say about this."

"Go ahead," I said.

"Meredith was trying so hard because she loves Todd. She's a great mom and a great wife! She's wonderful just like she is. Don't forget that when you talk about it later."

"I won't," I said.

And I didn't.

I've learned over the years that moms try hard because they really love their families. Their families appreciate the love, but they also love the mom in return and don't want to see her stressed out and overworked. And Meredith and other moms like her are never *really* Supermoms, because there's no such thing. They're only human . . . which is all we ask for.

---

# ♀AND A MOM WANTS YOU TO KNOW
## More About the Vicious Cycle of Guilt

As moms, we all know what guilt feels like. (As I was surprised to find out from Hogan in Chapter 4, dads are also very familiar with guilt.) I had a strange experience with guilt about the time my daughter turned one that I think some moms might relate to.

From the time my daughter was seven weeks old until she was seventeen months old, I worked forty hours a week—two days at the office and the rest from my house. As a musician, my husband worked nights and weekends, so he took care of her while I worked, and vice versa. At first, I felt guilty about leaving my baby on the two days I worked at the office, but after a few weeks, I saw that things were going well at home and my guilt dissipated. My husband cherished his time with the baby, and she loved being with her dad. I needed the break and started looking forward to the days I worked at the office.

But after a few months of feeling happy, a bad feeling began to set in. *Surely a truly good mom would not be happy leaving her little baby all day*, said a little voice inside of me, and the first wave of guilt washed over me. *You must be a very self-centered, cold person*, the voice added. *A good mom would be worrying constantly about her child.*

And so it began: I started feeling guilty for *not* feeling guilty! Despite the great progress my daughter was making and the happy smiles awaiting me when I came home from work, I began to worry that my absences had damaged her in some invisible and sinister way. My husband would be feeding her dinner when I came home and he'd give me the full report: cute things she'd done, highlights of her bodily functions.

"She didn't miss me too much, did she?" I'd ask, stroking her sticky hair while she played in her spaghetti.

"No, she had a great day," he'd say.

And then I'd practically throw myself at his feet and wail, "I'm sorry! I'm so sorry for being such a bad mother!"

"What are you doing?" he'd ask. "Get off the floor and go change out of your work clothes so I can leave, or I'll be late for rehearsal."

I'd do as he asked, but I'd feel bad the whole time. After a few weeks of this, he got tired of the drama. "Stop guilt-tripping yourself," he told me. "You're a great mom and everything at home is fine, but I'm starting to worry that you're too stressed out."

Until he said so, I hadn't realized I'd been guilt-tripping myself—that small voice was so deep in my subconscious that I hadn't realized what it had been saying. So I stopped guilt-tripping myself and I began to feel better and realize that my daughter was just fine, like my husband said.

Don't let yourself fall into a guilt cycle like I did. It can eat you up and stress everybody else out. (Remember, as Hogan explained in Chapter 4, your husband may be trapped in this cycle as well; if so, talk to him frankly and kindly to help him get out of it.) Don't feel guilty for not being a Supermom, or for not feeling guilty about not being a Supermom—just be yourself.

---

## Letting Go Is Healthy for Everyone

When you realize that Supermom is no more real than Wonder Woman, you can establish realistic expectations for yourself, and you and your family will feel more comfortable and relaxed. What should you do with any extra free time you have left over? You should find activities that don't involve housework or relate to your family. You can wallow in relaxation—take a hot bath, visit a friend, go to a movie—but after awhile you might get bored. That's when it's time to pursue more creative or constructive activities that validate you as a person, not as a mom or wife. Some examples are taking a photography class, learning yoga, volunteering (somewhere besides the elementary school), or keeping up on career skills if you're planning to go back to the work force.

Remember who you are as an individual, and your self-esteem will soar. You'll be giving your kids a great example, and you won't have to depend on your family for all of your validation and self-worth, which could get frustrating for you and annoying for them after awhile.

Someday, your kids will be grown up. While they'll always need you, they won't need your immediate time and attention like they do when they're little. When the time comes for them to be self-sufficient, you and they will be better able to handle the transition if you've kept up other interests. Personally, I have struggled with this as a stay-at-home dad. My teenagers are about to leave the nest! Of course I'm excited for them, but I'm dreading them leaving, and I know my life will never be the same once they're gone, even if they come back on so-called "financial recovery plans."

There is a silver lining, though, because I have my own passion to look forward to: sharing the information from the Proud Dads workshops and my own parenting experience to make the road smoother for other involved dads and moms than it was for Tina and me! I want you to have this feeling of satisfaction, too. Take the time to do things that interest you and remember that Supermom doesn't exist. As you'll see in the next chapter, neither does Superdad.

## Dad's Play-by-Play: What to Know from Chapter 8

- Supermom does not exist.
- Celebrities aren't Supermoms. Don't compare yourself to them.
- Watching their wives try to play Supermom is painful for dads. They feel very strongly that moms should cut down on the responsibilities they've set themselves up for, and

delegate some of those tasks to other people, or else let them slide altogether.

- Supermom ideals do not match up well with reality! Trying to be a Supermom can inflict too much pressure on yourself, your kids, your husband, and your bank account.

- Realize which of your tasks are really necessary and appreciated by your family, and drop what's not.

- Don't feel guilty about not being a Supermom. Also, if you've managed to avoid the guilt, feel good about your accomplishment instead of falling into a guilt cycle.

- If you have extra time left over, spend it on yourself by relaxing or pursuing outside interests that help you grow as an individual.

# ...AND WE CAN'T BE "SUPERDADS," EITHER

**I**n Chapter 7, I talked about the Bumbling Dad stereotype. As I illustrated there, those negative stereotypes can be very harmful to men. They're at the extreme end of the stereotype spectrum. At the other end is Superdad. Real Dad—a "Clark Kent" dad, if you will—is somewhere in the middle:

········································· The Dad Spectrum ·········································

**Bumbling Dad:** an inept doofus who can't do anything right

**Real Dad:** a regular guy who tries his best but sometimes makes mistakes

**Superdad:** a perfect dad who can do no wrong

The focus of this chapter is Superdad, square-jawed, cape flying in the wind as he stands atop a skyscraper, hundred-dollar bills swirling around him. Who is this mysterious masked man, and where did he come from?

The father archetype from 1950s sitcoms still forms our expectations of how dads should be in an ideal world. I think that today, TV shows like *Leave It to Beaver* are romanticized as a model we should always aim for but which we all know has been left hopelessly in the past. That leaves us all feeling like failures as family members and feeds our desire to do more, be more, and need more.

As we saw in the last chapter, moms are doomed to failure and frustration if they try to emulate so-called "Supermoms" from TV and the media. The same is true for dads: nobody can succeed if he's trying to do the impossible.

So who are the Superdads we saw in the past, and what have they become today?

The traditional Superdad stereotype was solidified in shows like *Ozzie and Harriet*, *Make Room for Daddy*, *My Three Sons*, *Andy Griffith*, *Courtship of Eddie's Father*, *Family Affair*, and *Father Knows Best*. In these shows, Dad was always around and very involved with the family, although he didn't wash dishes, do laundry, or partake of day-to-day childcare. In contrast, these guys had day jobs. In contrast to today's sitcom dads, they were wise—they *did* know best. Ward Cleaver, who is probably the most famous of these dads, often helped Beaver by giving him sound, moralistic advice that helped his son make the right decisions.

Today, I think that we laugh at these stereotypes behind our hands, but with some sense of wistfulness; there's a sense of longing for the days when life was so simple.

Of course, though, it wasn't. It was just written that way for TV.

The same thing happens today. A host of TV shows and movies show us ideal dads, but we have to remember that these characters are just that: characters, and nothing more.

If you take a look at current movies and TV shows, you'll see that today's Superdad has evolved a little since the TV shows I just mentioned. Let's check in with Superdad and see how he's doing these days. A day in the life of the modern Superdad goes like this:

Over breakfast, Superdad explains some complicated long division to his son before jumping in his sports car and taking the traffic-free shortcut to work that only he knows about. Swinging his briefcase and adjusting his tie, he takes the elevator to the top floor of his building, to his large, glass-walled office overlooking the city below. He has a mahogany desk, empty except for a blotter, a phone, and a framed picture of his family. It's not clear what Superdad does, although he spends his days making weighty decisions that affect thousands of employees across the nation. However, just because he lolls around the office and golf course all day doesn't make him a silver-spooned weakling. Underneath that suit and tie, Superdad's six-foot-two frame is a mass of rippling muscles, covered in just the right amount of body hair (don't tell anyone, but he waxes his back and shoulders).

The most important characteristic of Superdad's job is that he gets paid a lot. How much? We don't know, but it's enough to make an average American's dreams come true and then some. Enough for a big house in the best neighborhood, a vacation home, some corporate real estate, venture capital, successful stock holdings, a slam-dunk retirement, and enough savings for the kids' college tuitions all the way through medical school. Oh, and plenty of liquid cash to satisfy any whims he or his family might have.

For example, on this particular day, Superdad looks through his secretary's messages and sees a change in Monday's schedule. He calls home, and his wife stops her cheerful vacuuming to chat with him.

"Honey, what are you doing this weekend?" Superdad asks.

"Oh, the usual," she answers. "Lunch with my girlfriends and then I'm getting my nails done. Why?"

Superdad grins, showing even, white teeth. "Cancel."

"Cancel? Why?"

"I have Monday free. Let's take a little vacation to Hawaii. We can leave tonight after Joey's soccer game."

"Wonderful!" his wife gushes.

After he gets off work at 2:30, Superdad changes into khaki pants and a polo shirt and picks up his son and daughter from school. When he tells them about that evening's trip to Hawaii, there's much squealing in the backseat. He drives to the soccer field, where, as head coach, he leads Joey's soccer team to an exciting 3–2 victory. Afterward, he stops for takeout pizza, and when he bursts through the twelve-foot-high front door of his house, carrying a hot pizza box and surrounded by his two happy kids and the yellow Labrador that has rushed up to greet him, he shouts, "Honey! I'm home!"

His beautiful, slender wife comes running, throws her arms around him, and gives him a loving kiss.

While the family eats pizza and waits for the shuttle that

will take them to the airport, his daughter confides in him about a bully at school, and Superdad gives her advice to solve the problem. He keeps everyone laughing with his witty jokes and even sticks straws in his ears and pretends to be an alien to cheer his daughter up.

Life is good in fantasy land, isn't it? This doesn't happen in real life, though, and it doesn't happen for long in the movies, either. This is about the time for a monkey wrench to be thrown so the movie can take off. While Superdad is having a blast with his family, his boss is making plans to lay him off. Or the plane to Hawaii is hijacked. Or maybe his wife is really an undercover FBI agent and she disappears from the airport, making him think she's left him for another man. Any of these plots would work. After all, who wants to watch some guy be perfect for two hours? So he can resolve conflict faster than a speeding bullet—that isn't possible in real life.

You may be thinking that you wouldn't want to be married to Superdad. Not all of these ideals are necessarily what a woman would want. That's because the pressure to be "super" comes largely from society and not always from the spouse. For example, I know a guy named Gill whose wife hated his sports car and begged him to sell it. Even though he saw owning a fancy sports car as a part of his successful Superdad identity, she thought it was a waste of money and a magnet for speeding tickets. It goes to show you that the concept of Superdad isn't always envisioned equally by men and women.

I guess it would be fun to be Superdad. He's rich, buff, good-looking, smart, and funny. He drives a prestigious, fancy car. He can do anything, and he does everything right.

But I have no desire to be Superdad, because, like Supermom, he just doesn't exist. I'm happy being a mild-mannered Clark Kent kind of dad.

> Hogan's Slogan #48: "Superdad does not exist.
> Clark Kent is the mild-mannered reality."

## How the Superdad Myth Can Harm Your Family

The Superdad myth can harm you, your husband, and your kids when it sets standards that are impossible to achieve. As we saw in the chapter about Supermoms, there's a discrepancy between the ideals and what most people can realistically achieve.

| Ideal | Reality |
|---|---|
| Superdad earns mega bucks. | These jobs are few and far between. |
| Superdad has the buff body of a Mr. Universe. | Not every dad has a sculpted physique that can turn heads. |
| Superdad is always funny. | Nobody can be funny all the time. |
| Superdad easily explains homework and tough playground problems. | These issues usually take time and work to solve rather than simple explanations. |
| Superdad has time to coach soccer games at 3 p.m. and fly to Hawaii whenever he wants. | Most high-powered jobs keep you running at a pace that leaves little time for fun or family. |
| Superdad is perfect. | Nobody's perfect! |

As you can see, these ideals can be a little far-fetched. You and your husband will both be disappointed if you expect him to attain these ideals. Here's what dads say about this:

*I try to not to fall into the Superdad trap. But it's hard because of all the expectations placed on me by my boss, wife, and kids. They all expect to come first.*

*Sometimes I get caught up in trying to be a Superdad because my dad definitely wasn't, and I want to give my kids more than what I had.*

*I wanted to be a better dad than I had growing up, so I overextended myself. We got into debt and I couldn't sleep at night.*

*I know I sometimes bite off more than I can chew. It can end up biting me in the butt.*

*Nowadays, there's a lot of pressure to be a Superdad. Sometimes I think we're being pressured to compensate for other deadbeat dads or dads from a generation ago who weren't involved.*

If we expect perfection—if moms expect Superdads or dads expect Supermoms—then we're setting ourselves up for marriages filled with conflict, stress, and maybe even divorce.

So relax any Superdad expectations you have of your husband. It may sound like I'm contradicting what I said in Chapters 6 and 7, where I said to hand your husband more household and childcare responsibilities and believe that he can succeed at them. Let me clarify the difference:

1. *Do* expect your husband to do his fair share of nurturing and chores, depending on what's realistic in terms of his schedule. Believe in his ability to succeed at his tasks.
2. *Don't* expect your husband to embody a Superdad myth

that includes things he may not be able to provide, like a six-figure income, abs of steel, or sixty witty one-liners a minute. Don't expect perfection.

---

## ♀AND A MOM WANTS YOU TO KNOW

## Cinderella Part II

Imagine that the story of Cinderella doesn't end with the wedding. Imagine *Cinderella Part II: The Childbearing Years*. In *Part II,* Cinderella and Prince Charming get to know each other much better. After all, you can fall in love with *anyone* at a royal ball. Come to find out, Prince Charming is just a regular guy. Cinderella, too. After ten years of marriage, they have each gained about twenty pounds. They could use more exercise, say a walk through the forest or some rounds of archery. But with all of the kingdom's business to attend to, plus raising of the next generation of royalty, who has time? Prince Charming is often away from the castle, visiting other parts of the kingdom to make sure relations with the dukes stay stable. When he's home, he stays up until midnight most of the time, going over accounts with his tax collectors and trying to figure out how he'll feed the servants and the knights when a drought has left the kingdom with less grain than usual. To make matters worse, a duke form the North has encroached on the kingdom and messengers have sent word that he has troops prepared for battle. Then the king dies, leaving the prince with no choice but to take over the kingdom, polish his armor, and round up his troops for battle in the North. Wearing his armor, he enters Cinderella's chamber. "Gotta go, babe," he says.

Cinderella, who is weaving a new tapestry, is fed up with all of this gallivanting around the kingdom. "What? Don't go off to battle and leave the kids! You could be killed. And without the knights, we'll be vulnerable to any passing band of bandits!"

"Well, don't yell at me!" he says. "What am I supposed to do? Let the duke just take over the kingdom? You're the one who wants a new castle!"

"Because this one has a leaky roof!" Cinderella shouts. "Duh!"

"Then you leave me no choice!" Prince Charming shouts back, slamming the screen down on his helmet and turning on his heel.

"Fine, then, go!" Cinderella screams at his back. "I always manage just fine without you, anyway!"

That night, their oldest son runs off in the night to join his father on the battlefield.

Cinderella is at her wit's end trying to manage the castle and do the prince's financial work at once. She worries that her husband and son will be killed. When a wave of plague strikes the castle, putting half of its inhabitants—including the servants—out of commission, she finds herself mopping up vomit from the stone floor and screams, "This is not what I had in mind when I married Prince Charming!"

She has every right to be tired, frustrated, and disgusted, I'll agree. But it's not so much Prince Charming's fault as it is the result of life's foibles and circumstances. The same applies in the lives of real moms and dads everywhere. There are times when any married parent has had just about all they can take of financial stress, rebellious teenagers, and puke. It's part of being a parent, and should be part of our expectations from the time we decide to have kids.

At the end of the movie, Prince Charming comes back wounded, but alive and with a new perspective on life. He'll take some vacation time and go for more walks in the forest. Their son, now matured, takes over most of his father's duties. Cinderella decides to stay in the old castle and deal with the leaks. Violins and French horns play as the couple walk hand in hand in the forest.

I had a man in one of my classes who got divorced, and the Superdad myth caused a lot of the conflict that led to the divorce. James was a dad who lived in an apartment with his wife and two kids. He was only twenty-one when his first kid was born, and came to my class when he and his wife were expecting their second baby.

"I'm here because I don't know what else to do," he said during the introductions. "My wife and I are going to have our second baby, and I'm afraid we're not going to make it."

That got my attention!

James worked as a plumber. He would have liked to own his own plumbing business so that he could earn more money, but he didn't have enough experience yet to start his own business. And he didn't have enough money saved up, either. "But how am I ever going to get enough money saved up if I'm the only one working?" he agonized.

"What does your wife say about things?" one of the other guys asked.

"She doesn't understand," James answered. I could hear the bitterness in his voice. "She gets on my case about my weight, how much money I earn, my schedule—you name it, we argue about it."

Six months later, his wife had filed for divorce. He told me that his wife thought he was a failure. The Superdad myth had destroyed his marriage.

## Letting Go of the Superdad Myth: How You Can Help

The less money a dad makes, the more the Superdad myth can hurt, because finances are where a lot of the myth is centered. Take Raul, a dad in one of my workshops who was a cop in a so-so city. When his kids were born, he was new on the job and only made about $32,000 a year, although he had great health benefits for his family. The pay wasn't as much as he would have liked, and the risks of being a cop were also a burden: he knew he could be killed on the job.

"What should I do?" he asked the other men in the group. "We're scraping by. I'm working nights, so I'm a wreck and not much help to my wife. When my kids are awake, I'm usually asleep. We're never going to get ahead! We can't even buy a house right now. And what if I get—what if I get hurt on the job?" he asked, avoiding the unmentionable.

Nobody responded for a while. I don't think they envied his problems. Finally, I spoke up. "I think you're doing a great job," I pointed out.

He was. *He was doing all he could*. That's the best anyone can do.

Raul wrote me an e-mail a few years later. He'd stayed on the force long enough to earn some seniority. With that came a day shift and an increase in pay. "Everything is working out okay," he wrote. "I just wanted to say thanks for pointing out that giving my best was enough. Sometimes I think it's easy to forget that."

You can help your husband realize this about himself and let go of the Superdad myth by following these tips:

- Be financially responsible (see Chapter 4).
- Don't put a lot of importance on material goods.
- Focus on your husband's efforts, not outcomes.
- Praise him for his efforts—effort is what makes an MVP!

I said earlier in the book that I, as millions of kids do, dreamed of playing in the National Basketball Association, but it didn't pan out for a lot of reasons, some of which were in my control, but most of which I couldn't control—like an injury. A study by Art Young, director of Urban Youth Sports at Northeastern University's Center for the Study of Sports in Society, showed that one out of every 50,000 high school athletes will ever become a part of a professional team (*Ebony*, Walter Leavy, November 1998).

Another known fact is that not every professional athlete will reach superstar status like Michael Jordan, Larry Bird, or Magic Johnson. Nevertheless, every athlete on the roster plays a valuable role as members of their teams.

A man's chances to be a good father are much greater than his chances of being a professional athlete, yet most people are much more forgiving of a professional athlete falling short of perfection than they are of a father.

In Major League Baseball, the average hitting percentage of a player is under .300. That means each time a player goes to bat, he fails to hit the ball over 70 percent of the time! In the NBA a player's average field goal shot percentage is 40 percent to 45 percent, meaning the player's failure rate is above 50 percent! And in the NFL, a quarterback's average pass completion percentage is also around 40 percent to 45 percent. *The player's failure rate is again above 50 percent.* In all three of these scenarios, the failure rate is greater than the success rate.

Each time a baseball player stands at home plate for his next at bat the fans know ahead of time that he will fail over 70 percent of the time, yet they still cheer him on with words of encouragement.

Commitment to excellence, a motto of the NFL Oakland Raiders, is a great goal to have; however, it doesn't guarantee perfection. If it did, the Raiders would have a winning season and championship team every year.

I know many professional athletes who get so caught up in chasing the trophy and achieving superstar status that they lose sight of the main reason they chose their respective sport—for the love and fun of the game. If a man places too much emphasis on lofty and unrealistic ideals, he'll miss all the fun and rewards of being a good husband and father.

My basketball dream didn't come true and I'm okay with that because my successes and accomplishments as a father have far exceeded those I would have had as an NBA player. Most men won't become professional athletes, but all men have the potential to be good fathers.

If you ask our kids, I think they'll tell you that I didn't have to have the power to dodge bullets, leap tall buildings in a single bound, change the course of mighty rivers, or bend steel with my bare hands to impress them. All I had to do was be around for them, and that's made them happy.

My role as a stay-at-home dad also didn't follow the path most people would say leads to superstar status and front page news. Nevertheless, I'm proud and happy of what I've accomplished as a "Clark Kent" husband and father as well as the contributions I've made by helping other fathers be the best that they can be. I know Tina and the boys feel the same way.

## Dad's Play-by-Play: What to Know from Chapter 9

- Superdad does not exist.
- Sitcom and movie Superdads aren't real. Don't compare your husband to them.

- Real dads are neither Bumbling Dads nor Superdads, but somewhere in the middle. It's okay to be a "Clark Kent" dad.

- Help your husband let go of the Superdad myth.

- Superdad ideals do not match up well with reality! If your husband is trying to be a Superdad, he may be inflicting too much pressure on himself, the family, and the finances.

- Buying into the Superdad myth can set a dad up for failure and result in conflict, and even divorce.

# DADS ARE NOT MOMS

**M**oms and dads can and do parent differently, and that's fine. In any given marriage, the husband and wife are going to have differences that end up creating conflict. Are those differences a result of their biology—a result of the fact that she has a woman's brain and he has a man's brain? Or are they a result of how their parents raised them to fulfill their husband/father and wife/mother roles? Or a result of their personalities? Or of their cultures? Or the neighborhoods they grew up in?

I often read in the newspaper, magazines, and other sources that these questions are at the heart of many important scientific and academic debates and research projects. At the forefront of the studies and discussions are questions like *Why do people do what they do?* Is it nature, nurture, some of both? Or, in more metaphysical terms, is it fate, God, or personal will?

I'll leave these questions to the PhDs, scientists, and whoever wants to spend their time finding out the answer.

I feel that understanding why is irrelevant to a mom and dad learning how to work together as a parenting team. Heck, after nineteen years of marriage I still don't understand why Tina does the things she does as a mom or a woman. Sometimes she doesn't understand me either. Nevertheless, we don't lose sleep over it because we prefer to enjoy our lives as parents and a couple.

We feel it's more important for us to accept each other's differences and value what each of us brings to the family table as a mom and a dad.

Bottom line is, moms and dads parent differently. However, it doesn't mean that they can't parent together. Tina and I are living proof that it can be done, but it hasn't been without its challenges and struggles.

First of all, Tina and I came from such different backgrounds. It is said that opposites attract, and that is true in our case. Tina and I often laugh at how different we are and wonder how we ever manage to still be together. Tina is a blonde-haired, blue-eyed, petite Lutheran California woman. She is an introvert who hates to dance and can't handle being the center of attention. I'm a black-haired, tall, nondenominational Asian man. I'm also an extrovert who loves to dance and doesn't mind being the center of attention.

I was raised by a single working mother, as I told you in Chapter 5. Because my mom, Josie, worked two jobs to support me and my brother, Pete, she wasn't around much, and

I had to learn to stand up for myself. I also told you about the many difficult social and cultural challenges I had to overcome . . . all without a dad around for guidance. I graduated high school, but never went to college, and I never had a place we could call home.

Tina, on the other hand, lived a more stable life. She comes from a traditional upper-middle-class family with conservative values. Her mom, Mary Ann, and dad, George, were great parents and always around. They were married for fifty-five years before George passed away, and Mary Ann still lives in the house that she and George built in 1955. As a girl, Tina went to private Lutheran schools, had lots of friends, was a homecoming princess, and later went to Valparaiso University. It often seems as though we grew up in separate worlds.

To make matters more complicated, her father and I were like night and day. When we first met it was a scene out of *Guess Who's Coming to Dinner*. George and I would never have made good bookends! Besides our obvious racial differences, George was an introvert, a creature of habit, traditional in his thinking, passive, conservative, and even-tempered. I'm an extrovert, a risk taker, an assertive go-getter who thinks outside the box, and I have a short fuse.

Though Tina and I came from radically different backgrounds, I know that many other moms and dads feel like they come from a different world than their spouse.

To get a clearer picture of how deep our differences are, I drew up a list. Not all our differences are gender related. You might find it interesting to do the same and see just how many differences you and your husband have. Here's how my table looks:

|  | **Me** | **Tina** |
|---|---|---|
| **Sex** | Male | Female |
| **Race** | Half Dutch, half Indonesian | Anglo |
| **Class** | Lower | Upper middle |
| **Parents** | One mom, no dad around | Parents married fifty-five years |
| **Childhood neighborhood** | Impoverished, gang-infested | Stable suburb |
| **Education** | Some college | Bachelor's and master's degrees |
| **Personality** | Aggressive, risk-taker, not afraid to say what's on my mind, hard-nosed | Steady, caring, friendly, afraid to speak up, people pleaser |
| **Parenting style** | Involved; I push the kids to take risks and be adventurous | Involved; She warns the kids to use caution and think of how their actions affect others |

Take another look at the last row of the table. The key is to focus on how well our differences complement each other in a way that benefits our kids. For example, there are times when my leash on our boys is a little longer than Tina would like it to be. From Tina's point of view, it appears as though I'm placing our kids at risk of getting hurt. Then there are times when I feel Tina's leash is too short and that she is hurting our boys by being overprotective and babying them.

Neither is right or wrong, and both our perspectives serve a higher purpose. We work together in finding a happy medium that works for our family. There are times when Tina is there to remind me to tighten the leash on the boys to ensure their safety. Likewise, there are times when I'm there to remind Tina to loosen the leash on our boys to allow them the space they need to grow. The happy medium Tina and I agree on may be different from you and your husband's, and that's okay. What's important is that you and your husband find the happy medium that works best for your family. How do Tina and I accomplish this?

We use what I call the CCRs of parenting: Communication, Compromise and Rules of Engagement.

## Communication

Tina and I talk a lot, more than most couples. We constantly have in-depth discussions about issues like finances, religion, and parenting philosophies, topics that many couples avoid talking about. When we have these discussions, we don't take what the other person says personally. We realize it's just a point of view based on our role as a mom and dad. Therefore, we always keep the lines of communication open, and we make a point of thanking each other and paying each other compliments.

## Compromise

Tina and I both understand that there will always be conflict in our marriage, so we work very hard to always come up with a compromise.

What I mean by compromise is that in one case I may give in to Tina's method of dealing with our boys. If it doesn't work, we try my way. Sometimes her method is more effective and other times mine is. Then there are times when neither method works and we work together to find another solution.

## Rules of Engagement

Tina and I have established a set of rules on how to engage in a disagreement we have in raising our boys. Out of the three this has been the most challenging to follow through on. Emotions run high in the heat of the moment. But this is where Tina and I have learned a big lesson about keeping our composure. One good way to ensure there is no civil unrest during these discussions is to establish the following rule. The person who holds the Nerf ball (or any kind of soft item—a pot or a pan is not a good idea) gets to talk. And the other person must listen. When the person holding the Nerf ball is finished speaking they must hand it to the other spouse. Tina and I also established a rule to never discuss our different parenting styles in front of the children so as to not undermine each other. This was and still is a work in progress for us. It takes a tremendous amount of discipline to abide by the rules we've established. This alliance has benefited us and the kids. The boys see us as a solid team, and they can't pit us against each other or manipulate us because we parent as a team.

In order to get along with your husband, you don't always need to know *why* he does what he does. You just need to know that he *is* different from you and that it can be a good thing.

Some of the moms from the groups I've led have summed it up like this:

*My husband had a father who was very abusive and drank a lot. I was afraid that my husband would turn out to be just like his dad. I became overprotective of the kids and critical about the way Gary took care of them. It took a while for me to realize how my gatekeeper approach was harming the kids and keeping Gary and our children from bonding with each other.*

*Once I let go of the fears I had about my husband turning into my father, who was emotionally and physically abusive, I saw a huge change in his interaction with our kids. He became much more involved with the kids than I ever imagined he would. Now I feel guilty for all the time he lost with the kids because I was too scared to let him be a dad.*

*My husband didn't have a father in his life. Not knowing his father made it difficult for me to trust Kurt's instincts and way of doing things he did as a dad.*

*My dad was very abusive and emotionally distant. I found myself giving Jeff too many detailed instructions. I didn't realize that I was enabling him. Once I let go of my fears it became clear to me that Jeff was going to be a great dad.*

It's the balance of two parenting styles—whatever and whyever they are—that gives kids the stable foundation they need. As one dad said:

*I like to push my kids to their limits to see how far they can go. This gives me a way to measure my limits, too, on how hard I can be on them. My wife doesn't agree with my methods. Well, sometimes I don't agree with her methods, either. Then again, she's a mom. And I'm a dad.*

The last comment brings me to my next point:

## Kids Need a Mom AND a Dad

As you already know, I'm not a scientist. I don't have a PhD, or even a BA. I'm just a dad. I want my kids to go further academically than I did. But with my life experiences and the unique opportunities I've had to be a stay-at-home dad, I've learned a lot that I've shared with you in this book already. Now here's another life lesson I've learned: kids need their moms and their dads.

Research does in fact corroborate this, and we as parents know it in our hearts. Unless there's some other factor like abuse, adultery, or alcoholism going on that you just can't tolerate, it's best to stick together. In other words, don't get divorced over whose turn it is to clean the bathroom, how to clean it, or how it should look.

Now don't get me wrong: you *should* stand up for yourself, you *should* be vocal, you *should* insist that career, childcare, and chores be balanced in a way you can live with. I'm just saying that the daily irritations of these things can probably be solved if you follow what's in this book and has worked for many other couples. Most of these issues can be solved, so it is probably in your, your husband's, and your kids' best interests to make things work.

As we saw in Chapter 6, kids need the balance of two parents in their lives. Two different ways of operating don't necessarily have to be at odds. The idea is not to pigeonhole people into prescribed roles, but to highlight what works about having more than one parent involved in the kids' lives.

Hogan's Slogan #74: "Your husband
does not have a feminine side."

Before I was married in 1987, I remember women I dated asking me to show them my feminine side. This was a confusing time for me—I don't have a feminine side because I'm a man! Just because I care for my kids and enjoy being a loving parent does not make me feminine. I'm a stay-at-home dad, but still a man. I still love to eat a good steak, watch football, drink beer, smoke a cigar, play poker, and ride a motorcycle (preferably a Harley-Davidson). I still protect my family from harm's way and provide for them to the best of my ability. It's just that I do this in a different capacity most of the time.

To show you what I mean, think about this: when have you ever heard a man ask a woman to show him her masculine side? If a working woman lands a big contract, can you imagine her coworkers praising her efforts by saying, "Hey, Suzy, now we're getting to see your masculine side!"? If a woman is a CEO, owns a company, or is enlisted in the military, that doesn't make her less of a woman.

I never asked any of the girls I dated to show me their masculine side. Nor have I ever asked Tina. I wouldn't want her to. One of the things I love about my wife is she's a *woman*. I respect Tina's differences and I think that they are important because together we make one heck of a good team, and I don't mind saying it! I am happy to share work and do what's best for our family, even when that means trading in my career and staying home to raise our kids, but I am still a man and she is still a woman. Neither of us considers the other's sex a drawback to who they are as a person. The end result is a healthier home life for the kids—and for us, too.

I will never forget one mom's group I facilitated a few years back. This group of women was very lively, curious, and excited to learn more about a father's perspective. I pointed out and gave examples of how moms can unknowingly and unintentionally undermine and discourage a father's involvement and enable his lack of involvement. One example I gave was something as simple as signing a gift, sympathy, get well or holiday card.

Early in our marriage, Tina would sign my name on cards she sent out to relatives and friends in her handwriting. Tina thought she was doing a good thing by not bothering me with the task of signing the card. I told her that I felt left out of the process and that I should sign my own name because we're a team. Furthermore, I had to be held accountable for signing my own name. This is an example in which it's okay to challenge a husband. How long will it take for him to sign his name? A few seconds. If he can't take a few seconds to be involved with signing a card, how can he be involved in his family and household?

Some people think this is trite. But women often are frustrated when men don't notice small details. For example, I can share lots of stories in which Tina got upset at me because I didn't pay attention to detail or forgot something about a memorable moment we had together. Sometimes I've failed to notice that she did something different with her hair or added a decorative item to the house. I've forgotten what she wore on our first date. I've also forgotten to buy a card for her birthday (it only happened once, and boy did she ever make me feel bad about it!)

A few days after I conducted the mom's workshop, I received a beautiful 8½-by-11-inch card with notes from every mom in attendance expressing their gratitude for giving them some valuable insight on a father's perspective. I was very touched by the card because it was personalized by each mom and I could feel the sincerity behind each word they had written. The card was intended to make me feel good, and it did. It would not have had the same meaningful impact on me if one mom had signed the card and then listed the other names in her handwriting. Here is one of the notes I received that best describes the content of the thank-you card.

> *I feel the number one benefit I personally got from your talk was understanding how my actions/words/reactions could be sabotaging my husband's efforts to be the dad he wants to be. A dad is not a mom. That isn't a bad thing—to not be a mom. For a father not to be a dad is a bad thing.*

The goal of team parenting is not to manipulate dads into doing exactly what a mom would do in any given situation. It's to have dads and moms involved and working together!

## Raising Tomorrow's Parents

Somebody once said about parenting, "The days are long, but the years are short." It's true—I can't believe that I'm on the home stretch now, with three teenagers, one who has already left home and is attending Pepperdine University. No matter how hard it is to be a parent, it's a fleeting state. One day soon, your kids will be grown, gone, and starting families of their own. While your day-to-day work may be largely over, and you'll see the laundry diminish and find yourself cleaning the bathroom less often, you will still be hard at work . . . in your kids' subconscious.

### Hogan's Slogan #103: "You remain frozen in time in your kids' subconscious."

Immortality redefined: all of these day-to-day issues and how you handled them will be forever imprinted on your kids' minds. When they become the parents of the next generation, I hope that our generation will have solved some of these tough questions about parenthood and roles so that they have less conflict in their marriages than our generation has seen and thus use more of their time to enjoy being parents. It's important to let the fathers and mothers of tomorrow see us treat each other fairly and kindly on a daily basis, no matter how hard our days are.

It's important for our sons and daughters to see fathers who are involved in their families. In some families, that means the father takes on a traditional breadwinning role; in other families—like mine—he may be the primary caregiver. It's important for sons and daughters to see that masculinity is multi-faceted and that it is okay for men to love their families and to show that love.

It's also important for our sons and daughters to see mothers who are fulfilled and happy. They need to view women not as household servants but as partners who contribute valuable ideas and morals to the family and the world, and who have the right and the ability to work outside the home. They need their moms to show them, with love, that men are valuable. When they choose a wife, they will be able to see value in women who have many different abilities—ultimately, abilities that complement their own.

Daughters also need this female role model. Some daughters will see their mothers working outside the home; others will not, but they need to see that their lives can go beyond their front doors, and that mothers and their love are a valuable part of society.

Also, daughters need to see their fathers as men who appreciate and value their wives. A father's love is instrumental in teaching a daughter how to choose a husband who values her and whose abilities complement her own.

Long after they're grown, your family reaps the benefits of your efforts today. So it's important to take stock now of how you approach your parenting on a day-to-day basis. Here are some tips for giving your kids good role models:

- Handle conflicts with grace and love.
- Never badmouth or undermine your husband in front of the kids. (For example, "Your dad is getting on my nerves," or "Don't listen to your dad. He doesn't know what he's talking about.")
- Never promote stereotypes of men or women in front of the kids. (For example, "Men are lazy pigs," or "Mommy will fix your lunch. Mommies are just better at cooking.")
- Balance the work in a way that's fair for your family.
- Encourage your husband to get involved with the kids.
- Model the behavior you'd want your kids to show as adults, because that's exactly what they're going to do.

I have to hand it to Tina for accepting how important it was not only for our kids but for *me* to be a father to our boys. She sees the bigger picture and how our different parenting styles as a mom and dad will prepare them for and benefit the relationship-building experience our boys will have with their future wives. No, this is not a guarantee that our boys will have a successful marriage and family. But Tina and I will grow older knowing we did the right thing by allowing each other to be who we are, a mom and a dad, to our children.

Tina and I are proud of what we've accomplished and know that our boys have learned a lot by watching us work together as a team.

Our boys may or may not choose to marry and have children of their own, but if they do, I know the parents of our daughters-in-law will find great comfort in knowing that their future sons-in-law were raised in an environment that showed them how to respect and accept their wives' differences and demonstrated how husbands and wives should act and work together in raising their children. This is the best gift we can give to our future daughters-in-law.

**Hogan's Slogan #131: "Helping fathers benefits mothers and children. And the next generation."**

I hope that this book will inspire you to become an active advocate for fathers. Why? Because the parenting landscape is not as father-friendly as you might think. This is easy to prove by taking a moment to step inside your husband's shoes.

If you were your husband and had some concerns about being a father, is there an accessible place in your community you could go to for help and support? I think you'll quickly discover that there is very little or usually nothing available for fathers, and that whatever *is* available is not comparable to the services available to mothers, as you saw when I told you about the hospital survey in Chapter 2. I'm certain that if the numbers were reversed, women would have something to say about it and would demand comparable services.

The best way for me to stress the significance of advocating support services for fathers is to address all the moms who have daughters. One day your daughter will probably fall in love with a little boy who is growing up today. They will marry and decide to have a child, which will make you a proud grandmother. When that time comes, would you like to have a fathering program available for your son-in-law that will help him be the best husband for your daughter and the best father for your grandchild? If so, then you need to act now.

One way to act is to write a letter urging hospitals in your community to provide a monthly program for fathers facilitated by a man. I've provided a sample letter in the appendix of this book for you to use when writing to hospitals (see p. 189). Collect signatures from other moms and submit the letter to the hospital administrators.

I'm passionate about fatherhood—not just because I love our children but also because I feel a responsibility to prepare them for their possible role as husbands and fathers. I also feel I have a social responsibility to help as many fathers as I can.

Although I believe most men want to be good dads, there are a lot of vulnerable dads out there who are either ambivalent or unaware of how to go about taking that first step into being an involved father. They continue to fall short of their goal to be good husbands and fathers, not because they lack the desire but rather because they lack the resources and support. I call these men ONA-OFFA Dads (on again–off again) who constantly fall off the daddy track and spend more time working to get back rather than staying on the track. Their efforts are spent trying to repair relationships rather than build them.

The best way to help these dads is to help them help each other. The best way to accomplish this is to educate moms and to provide readily accessible open discussion forums where these fathers can gather.

As with moms, the best resource a father has is other fathers. I know this because during my stay-at-home dad tenure I had the unique opportunity of being a part of a stay-at-home mom's group. These moms were gracious and kind enough to include me in their morning coffee sessions, afternoon playgroups, luncheons, and yes, even a "white elephant" Christmas party. I learned a lot from these moms and they became a valuable resource for me, and a great support group, too! They were instrumental in helping me be the best husband and father I could be to my family. If moms can have this kind of intimate camaraderie and networking forum available at a moment's notice that helps them become better mothers, why can't dads? There is a lot that fathers can teach other fathers.

I hope that you and your family live the life that's right for you. I hope that you experience life to the fullest and that you, your husband, your kids, and your marriage are not perfect, but happy, stable, and fulfilling.

## Dad's Play-by-Play: What to Know from Chapter 10

- We don't know for sure what determines our behavior, but we know that individual men and women tend to parent differently.

- Differences can complement each other instead of causing conflict.

- Kids can benefit from Dad's parenting style as much as they can from Mom's.

- Your husband does not have a feminine side.

- Your kids will benefit from seeing both mom and dad parenting together as a team.

- The payoff will come years from now—but sooner than you expect!

- Your kids are the parents of tomorrow.

# Conclusion

Now you've learned ten secrets that men have shared with me since 1992, and how you can use your new knowledge to make your married life and your family life easier, happier, and more fulfilling. I hope this knowledge reduces some of the conflict and stress in your marriage so that you, your husband, and your kids have more time and energy to enjoy all that life has to offer.

As you engage in team parenting, go easy on yourself, because it's not easy. Being a "successful" family—that is, a family in which everyone's basic needs are met, including yours—is about the good, the bad, and the differences, and it takes hard work. If you need to quantify it at all, measure your success as parents by how you worked through your differences and difficulties, rather than by your financial or public accomplishments. Parenting mistakes are inevitable. *Remember, there are no perfect parents.*

Someone once asked me, "Hogan, what's the difference between a good dad and a bad dad?"

I replied, "A good dad never gives up on himself, his wife, and his children." This could also be said with respect to moms. I ask that you not give up on yourself, your husband, or your children.

I extend my warmest wishes to you and congratulate you for being a parent who cares!

# Appendix: Sample Hospital Letter

You can use this letter to request an expectant dads' class at your local hospital or community education center.

Dear _____,

I am a member of the community and my husband would like to attend a class for new and expectant fathers. He is interested in the topic and excited about becoming a dad, but he doesn't have a lot of resources. He needs an open discussion forum where he can learn from other dads and express his fears, frustrations, and worries about his role as a father in today's world.

Would you please arrange for a workshop? Please feel free to contact me if you have any questions.

Thank you,


[Your name]
[Your phone number and/or e-mail address]

# For Further Reading and Online Interaction

## Books

- *Embracing Your Father: How to Build the Relationship You've Always Wanted with Your Dad*. Dr. Linda Nielsen (McGraw-Hill, 2004).
- *The Expectant Father*. Armin A. Brott and Jennifer Ash (Abbeville Press, 2001).
- *Nonviolent Communication: A Language of Compassion*. Marshall B. Rosenberg, PhD (Puddledancer Press, 2002).
- *The Proper Care and Feeding of Marriage*. Dr. Laura Schlessinger (HarperCollins, 2007).
- *VoiceMale: What Husbands Really Think About Their Marriages*. Dr. Neil Chethik (Simon & Schuster, 2006).

## Websites and Blogs

- www.momsguidetodads.com. The official site for this book. Learn more about us, or contact Hogan.
- http://whatmomswantdadstoknow.blogspot.com. Join our discussion with other readers of this book!
- http://menbehavingdadly.blogspot.com. Here's our blog for dads—tell your husband!
- www.pregnancy.com. For expectant moms.
- www.robynsnest.com. An interactive resource for moms.

# Acknowledgments

We are extremely grateful to the following individuals and organizations who have made this book possible:

First, our wonderful and hardworking agent Laurie Harper, whose insight and wisdom guided us from start to finish; Ron Pitkin and Cumberland House for believing in the book and giving it a place to call home; Dr. Laura Schlessinger, for her goodwill and support; Dr. Neil Chethik and Dr. Linda Nielsen for their enthusiasm and support; Dr. Jeff Jones and Chuck Flacks, for opening their workshop to a female observer; soon-to-be Dr. Alyssa Crittenden for anthropological insights and reading material; Dr. Gloria Sklansky, may she rest in peace, for the clearest explanation ever of assertive behavior; Dr. Kathleen Nickerson for insight into how people get along and what motivates them. We also would like to thank the many moms and dads whose voices, through their stories and comments, have made this book so real.

Finally, we would like to thank our spouses and children for their love and support during the writing and always. We love you!

## About the Authors

**Hogan Hilling** is the founder of Proud Dads, Inc., through which he develops and conducts expectant father classes for hospitals in Southern California and conducts workshops on fathering issues throughout the United States. The author of *The Man Who Would Be Dad* and the father of three boys, he and his wife, Tina, live in Newport Beach, California. He can be reached through his website, www.momsguidetodads.com.

**Jesse Jayne Rutherford** is a mother, freelance writer, and writing coach. She is the coauthor of *Speaking Up: How to Help the Children You Work With Who Live in Abusive Homes* and the coauthor of *Save the Date: A Curriculum for Teens on Developing Healthy Dating Relationships*, which she wrote on staff at the Family Violence Project. She and her husband and daughter live near San Diego, California. She can be reached through her website, www.jesserutherford.com.